F-O-R-E-W-A-R-N-E-D

You won't believe everything in this book. You shouldn't. Like all of Gaul, it is divided in three parts: Truths, half truths and fabrications. It is to your amusement to determine which part is which.

This book will tell you about Montana's fur-bearing fish. How to forecast weather by pigs' spleens. How Henry Plummer, the infamous road agent and sheriff, might have escaped hanging.

How Jim Bridger and John Colter might have handled TV interviewers.

You will learn about a lady of the night who provided curb service for sheepherders.

Read about a taxi dance hall girl who set a world's beer drinking record during the Fort Peck dam construction days.

Montanans can be humorous. They tell tall tales. Make jokes. Poke fun at themselves.

As Victor Hugo so aptly portrayed it: "Laughter is the sun that drives winter from the human face."

MONTANA'S BRAND OF WESTERN HUMOR

BY ALBERT ERICKSON

HELENA, MONTANA

To Montana Pioneers...

This book is dedicated to the residents of Montana who endured stage coach robbers, hangings, Indian wars, cattlemen-sheepmen disputes, drouths that broke dryland farmers and their banks, the woes of the Great Depression and the recent closing of major industries. Despite these adversities, Montanans never lost their sense of humor or ability to enjoy a good story.

Contents

Acknowledgments 7
Quips and Quirks
    From Vigilantes to Calamity Jane 8
Ham and Wry
    Bald-Headed Rustler, Flatulent Horses, Sex by the Mile,
    Outhouse Decorum, Turning Off Old Faithful 9
Cowboys' and Sheeperherders' Hi Jinx
    Curb Service for Sheepherders, Eggs Sunnyside Up, High
    Stakes Poker 15
Go with the Flow
    Glimpses from the Virginia City Golden Gulch 17
1889—The Year That Wuz
    100-year-old Newspaper Items from Sharp-Shooting Editors. . . 20
Boodle, Booze & Silk Stockings
    The Helena and Anaconda Fight for the State Capital 22
You'll Know You're in Montana When 27
All Sorts of Things and Weather
    Weather Forecasting by PS, Weather Whoppers, Earthquakes
    Sire Mirthquakes 28
Whimsical Map of Montana
    Amusing Oddball Out-of-the-Way Places to be Found
    in the Big Sky Country 31
The Beforehands
    Artist Charlie Russell and Other Humorous Montanans 36
Once Over Easy
    Fur-Bearing Fish, Cowboy Dancers, Laughs Among the Lewis
    and Clark Expedition, A Forest of Distinction 40
Bottom Fishing
    The Fishing Caste, Are Fishermen Habitual Liars? 48
Rugged Individuals, We Are Us
    Misconceptions of Montana and Montanans, Profiles of
    Montana Characters 50
In Western Vernacular
    Montana Glossary, Do's and Don'ts in the Big City 55
With Tongue in Cheek
    How to Bruise Montana History and Its Characters:
    Sheriff Henry Plummer, Mountain Men Jim Bridger
    and John Colter 58
Foofaraws, or Ornamented Stories
    Boom Town Taxi Dancers, Valley of 10,000 Haystacks,
    The Outriders, Loot of the Innocents. 63
At Trail's End
    The Fun Bunch. 79

Acknowledgments

I traveled Montana extensively for fifteen years and in my wanderings I came across some wonderful storytellers. To them I am grateful, and also to the many others who contributed and made possible this publication.

Dave Walter, Montana Historical Society research librarian.

Jack Cooper Russell, California, son of C. M. Russell.

Bart McDowell, senior editor of *National Geographic*.

A. B. Guthrie, Jr., Choteau, Montana, novelist.

Dick Pace, Virginia City historian and contributor to this book.

Ken Byerly, Lewistown publisher and friend of the late Joe Montgomery.

Bert Lindler, outdoor writer on the staff of the Great Falls *Tribune*.

Mrs. June Tatsey, in-law of John Tatsey, the Blackfoot Indian policeman whose writings were admired by Senator and Ambassador Mike Mansfield.

Dick Wheeler, author and faculty member of Eastern Montana College of Education, a critiquer at a Montana Writers conference.

Barbara Fifer, Helena, book editor who did a superb job in correcting my grammar and punctuation, but not spelling. There I am letter perfect.

Mark Thompson of American Geographic Publishing for his advice in preparing the script.

Quips & Quirks _____

Montana's history is filled with humorous quips and quirks. In *Montana: A State Guide Book* (Federal Writers' Project of the Works Projects Administration, 1939)will be found a number of interesting sidelights.

A posse of 21 men from Alder Gulch rode into Hell Gate, near the present site of Missoula, and rounded up several road agents who had been fingered by the Vigilantes, a voluntary citizens' organization formed to bring law and justice to the territory.

After brief trials, one of the purported road agents, George Shears, was hanged in a barn. He was instructed to climb a ladder up to the noose to save the trouble of preparing a drop for him.

At the top of the ladder Shears said, "Gentlemen, I am not used to this business. Shall I jump off or slide off?" He was told to jump off.

Calamity Jane was known in the Old West as one tough female, but she met more than her match in Livingston, Montana when she tangled with Madame Bulldog Kitty O'Leary, who ran what the *Montana Guide* termed "what was euphemistically known as a dance hall." The Bulldog tipped the scales at 190 and served as her own bouncer.

She and Calamity Jane were bosom buddies, but they had a falling out, whereupon Madame Bulldog tossed Calamity Jane into the street. "Easy as licking three men," she said.

When asked if Calamity tried to fight back, a bystander replied, "Calamity was tougher than hell, but she wasn't crazy."

It seems that a respectable citizen in Miles City hit a gambler on the head with a singletree and killed him. To save the good man embarrassment, his friends hastily hanged the dead man as "a dangerous character."

Thomas J. Dimsdale, in his book *The Vigilantes of Montana* (published in Virginia City by D.W. Tilton, 1882), described a number of residents of Montana and their idiosyncrasies.

One was Gus Graeter, who Dimsdale states was an industrious man and did much toward the upbuilding of southwestern Montana. He mined, built ditches, was a merchant and a county officer, built an electric light plant for Dillon, was a banker and always an early riser.

Chris Snyder, a Graeter employee, says that when Gus was on the ranch he would get up before daylight, go into the hen house and cuss the roosters because they did not crow early enough to wake the hired men.

Then there was the new editor of *The Vociferator* (how's that for the name of a newspaper?) who placed this slogan on the masthead of his paper: "We did not come to Montana for our health."

Coming Day, of Fort Belknap reservation, was known for his bravery at more than 80 years of age. In 1936, according to *Montana: A State Guide Book*, he boarded the white man's "thunder bird," during the reservation's fair, and waved to his quaking comrades. When the plane was several thousand feet up, he shouted to the pilot in the Gros Ventre tongue to go higher.

"As yet," he hollered scornfully, "we are not to the height where flies the common magpie."

Ham & Wry _____

Bald-Headed Rustler

Bannack, Montana's first gold strike town and its first territorial capital, was a dusty crowded mining camp, filled with "get rich quick" adventurers from the gold fields of California and other places, along with the usual camp followers of gamblers, prostitutes and hangers-on.

With the population constantly rising, merchants' offerings were in great demand. A nearby Grasshopper Valley rancher, who shall remain nameless, decided ranching was too slow, so he opened a butcher shop in Bannack and prospered from the start.

Beef, red meat, is what the hard-working miners wanted. He couldn't keep up with the demand, but he had a real neat idea as to how he could augment his supplies.

As night came on, he would ride out to Bannack ostensibly to visit his Grasshopper Valley ranch. Instead he rode out onto the range and rounded up stray cattle that he came across. Brands didn't matter—it was too dark to read them.

As he told me the story in 1939: "Things went along swimmingly. I was taking in gold dust by the poke. One thing irked me, though. I was getting bald headed from all my night riding."

"How come?" queried a bystander.

"I didn't want anyone to get suspicious. When I rode out of town, instead of having my lariat hanging on the pommel, I wound it up and placed on my head under my ten gallon hat.

"Guess all that riding bounced the rope up and down and caused my hair to fall out.

"Then one moonlit night there came a reckoning. I accidentally looked at the brand and found out I was rustling my own cattle. That's when I quit being a butcher and took up ranching steady."

Mash-Sniffing Horse Assisted Revenuers

Much has been made about dogs that can sniff out marijuana, or canines that comb avalanches to determine locations of buried persons.

During Prohibition, Revenuers made use of a "mash-sniffing" horse to locate hidden stills.

The horse was owned by a rancher in the Centennial Valley, located in southwestern Montana. He was called Stubby because, while a colt, both ears had been frozen into stubs.

What he lacked in ears, he made up in smeller. He had an uncanny ability to smell sour mash half a mile away.

The Centennial is a broad valley with lots of draws and canyons in which the moonshiners hid their stills. But Stubby could smell them out, much to the delight of the Feds of the Alcohol Tax Unit.

Stubby had a weakness. After he sniffed out the mash, he loved to eat it. You could ride Stubby to a still, but you had to walk him home.

Stubby lies in an unmarked grave. Too bad there isn't a headboard that reads:

Here Lies Stubby
Died in Devotion to Duty
—*contributed by Harry Cosgriff, Helena*

There Are Limits to Fish Limits

A city feller, maybe a tourister, stopped at a ranch to find out how the fishing was.

The rancher said, "Good." He directed him to his young son who was fishing down at the creek.

As the would-be angler neared the creek, he saw a boy come out of a Chic Sales house (outhouse to you) with a string of nice-looking fish.

The eager fisherman asked where he had caught the string of fish. "In there," said the lad, pointing to the outhouse. "Come on I'll show you."

Inside was a two-holer and since the outdoor facility jutted over the creek, he could see several trout swimming in the pool below.

"Here, take my pole," offered the rancher's son. "You can catch your limit in no time."

Despite the fact the outhouse was abandoned, the city angler responded, "Thanks, but no thanks."

Not having the stomach for that kind of fishing, he decided to try fishing another day at another place.

Flatulent Horses Are a Nuisance

In an explosive decision, the Montana Supreme Court, not too many years ago, ruled that dude ranchers cannot keep Belgian draft horses in a subdivision of a resort community near Yellowstone National Park.

Lawyers for the resort association argued before the court that the horses expelled gas in such a noisy way as to disturb the peace and quiet of the mountain development.

"These horses and their ensuing resounding, egregious divestitures of abdominal gas echoing through the hills and vales of this otherwise peaceful area, closely akin to the point blank discharge of a double barreled shotgun, have utterly no place in this quiet, residential hamlet..." quoted an Associated Press dispatch.

To which a justice of the Montana Supreme Court responded, "While the loquacious author is guilty of hyperbole, the nuisance premise is difficult to dispute."

A Helena newscaster capped the story by stating, "Guess that is why they are called draft horses."

Sex by the Mile

Back in the mining heyday, there were companies that operated on a grand scale.

One such was located in southwestern Montana. It had a community of its own, bunk houses, cook shack and a church. There was even a narrow gauge railroad for hauling out the ore.

Its management and principal stockholder was an impressive man. Not only was he a mining mogul, but he was a master of raising mining financing.

Periodically, he would head back East to refinance his operations. Seeking money to buy new machinery, repair the railroad or for exploratory purposes, he would invariably return with a new "grubstake."

His method was to sell bonds to wealthy ladies and gentlemen who were eager to cash in on the West's mining boom.

One evening, while on a train out of New York City, he told me that a conductor approached him in the club car asking if he would like female companionship.

I said, "Is she expensive?"

"It depends," the conductor said, "she charges by the mile."

"My, oh my," I replied looking at the landscape whizzing by. "I wish I had that lady on my narrow gauge train out in Montana. It would cost me hardly nothing."

A Fly Is a Fly Is a Fly

We had a justice of the peace in our hometown who was a sagacious cuss.

He had seen many a witness on the stand who got his or her comeuppance at the hands of a smart attorney.

One day he found himself on the witness stand during a hearing about closing a stockyard which was termed a public nuisance.

As communities do, they tend to grow—and this one had almost circled the stockyard. Residents of the neighborhood were complaining about the multitude of flies in the area.

The J.P's home was about three blocks from the stockyards. When queried about flies at his place by the stockyard's attorney, he replied, "Yes, there are flies at my place."

"Are there more flies than usual?"

"Oh, I don't know."

"Do you think they come from the stockyards?" asked the attorney.

"Cain't rightly tell where they come from," he said, "none of them are branded."

In a cattle country courthouse that brought forth a huge guffaw.

When Exposure Is Not Exposure

Judges, or justices of the peace, in their decisions can indulge in side-splitting witticisms at times.

Such was the case in a small town of western Montana. The occasion was a rodeo or Fourth of July celebration which brought out a crowd that patronized the bars until closing time.

As the celebrants began the parting of their ways, they noted a man and his wife relieving themselves alongside Main Street.

A constable seeing the act arrested them. They were arraigned the next day before a J.P. noted for his drollery.

After hearing the constable's testimony, the J.P. fined the man $25 for indecent exposure and dismissed the wife's charge.

When the judge was asked why he didn't fine the woman, he replied, "She didn't show anything."

Outhouse Decorum

Numerous versions of this early-day incident have been attributed to several individuals. It has been repeated so often that it has become a western classic.

The setting is a small Montana town with its usual combination restaurant and saloon. Where there was a saloon there had to be an outhouse or outhouses to serve both sexes.

The aforementioned establishment was a duplex outhouse with His and Hers labeled with signs above the respective doors.

As the night wore on an itinerant patron asked the bartender "Where's the can?"

"Out the back door," the bartender replied. The drunk staggered into the outhouse, forgetting to close the door. As he sat there, a shot came out of the darkness and dirt flew in his face.

Silhouetted in the saloon door stood a huge man who bellowed, "Get the hell out of there, you're sitting on the ladies' side."

It could have happened anywhere in the West—the six-shooter was a great mover of men.

Disposable Razors

Hal Stearns, former publisher of the Harlowton *Times,* recounts the following story, which he says appeared in the Meagher County *News* at White Sulphur Springs, Montana.

Fred Ward, editor and owner of the paper, noticed a light late in the evening in the town's mortuary. Sensing a story, he went to investigate. He met a barber coming out of the mortuary.

Ward said, "What are you doing in the mortuary at this late hour?"

"I was shaving one of the undertaker's customers." Fred was curious and queried, "What do you charge to shave a dead man?"

"Ten dollars," replied the barber.

"That's pretty steep when you only charge a live customer fifty cents." "Yeah, I know but I have to throw away the razor after I shave a dead man."

That ended the conversation, but Fred couldn't let it rest, he added a postscript to the story. "I wonder, did he really throw away that razor?"

Turning On and Off Old Faithful Geyser

As everyone knows, the world's most famous geyser, Old Faithful, is in Yellowstone National Park.

The Washburn-Langford expedition exploring the Yellowstone area in 1872 came upon Old Faithful and described it as "a great, white, scalding edifice—a geyser—a great, magnificent geyser."

With the advent of automobiles, millions drove to the Park to see the phenomenon of Old Faithful.

In the early '20's era of the "gear jammers," who drove Yellowstone Park busses, and other employees called "savages," crowds would pack the area in front of Old Faithful waiting for the subterranean rumblings that presaged its eruption.

Two of the "savages" decided to jazz up the geyser's hourly performances.

They found a cart wheel and proceeded to mount it on top of a pole near Old Faithful. One of them manned the wheel while his partner would station himself in front of the crowd. At the most propitious moment he would cry out "Okay. Turn 'er on!"

After a few more rumbles and false spurts, tons of white steaming water would rise a hundred or more feet to prove its claim of the world's highest geyser.

The crowd would remain silent and awestruck until a spectator was heard to say, "How about that? They can turn it on and off."

How many of the fake eruption-controlled performances the pseudo-engineers made is not a matter of record.

—Contributed by Ernie Neath, Helena

Humor in Death Certificates

Humor can be found in the oddest places. Several Montana dailies carried the following death certificate laughers.

"Went to bed feeling well but woke up dead." Or the one about a robust citizen who died suddenly: "Deceased had never been fatally sick."

There was one of a blacksmith who died as the result of injuries sustained while shoeing a horse. It bore the following notation: "Kicked by a horse shod on the left kidney."

Then there was a doctor who wrote on a death certificate, "Do not know cause of death, but patient fully recovered from last illness."

It's possible, but not probable, that a vital statistics clerk might have laughed himself to death while examining death certificates.

Cowboys' and Sheepherders' Hi-Jinx

The Sheepherders Loved It

Beaverhead County, a few decades ago, was big sheep country. Where there were sheep, there were sheepherders. Where there were sheepherders, there were hookers.

Back in the prime of sheep raising, sheepherders were an economic plus for the Dillon merchants. After months on the range, they were not only seeking wine, women and song, but they were in need of wearing apparel—pants, shirts, shoes and jackets.

For the free spenders, often the first stop was at a men's apparel store where they would deposit a hundred dollars or so and make the merchant promise not to give them any of the money regardless of how drunk they were or how many floozies they brought into the store. That was their sacred clothes money.

Small communities have reformers and such a movement swept through Dillon, forcing the authorities to ban prostitutes. The flesh embargo didn't last long. It was the merchants who petitioned the city authorities for their return—too many of the sheepherders were taking the train to Butte or Idaho Falls.

Some of the gals were fixtures in the town. One, in particular, was called "dirty mouth" because of her foul language. She had more expletives than a Marine drill sergeant.

One day I came across her in a jewelry store where she was waiting to get her watch checked. She struck up a conversation by saying, "Jeez, I'm tired."

I bit and said, "How come?" I was curious also. "You know," she said, "sheepherders can't get to town very often so I have instituted a drive-around service. I go out to their sheep wagons and business sure has been booming."

And so was born a new business, curb service for sheepherders.

Sheepherders' R&R

Two Norwegian sheepherders were in Big Timber for rest and recreation after being out on the range for months tending sheep.

The first part of the R&R was recreation, which meant a stop for liquid refreshments. The rest part occurred if and when they passed out.

While they were tossing off a few, a Salvation Army woman

entered the saloon seeking donations. She used the same approach on all prospective contributors.

When she confronted the two sheepherders, she inquired, "Have you been saved? Have you found Jesus?"

Lars turned to her and said, "Vat, is *He* lost again?"

—*contributed by Chris Boe, Billings*

Eggs, Sunnyside Up, or Else

I was a witness to this in a Montana small-town cafe.

An inebriated cowboy sat at the counter and ordered ham and eggs, the eggs over. In due time the waitress brought him the meal. After eating half of it, the drunk cowpoke discovered that the eggs were turned over.

He bawled out the hasher, telling her he ordered them sunnyside up. She argued that is the way he ordered them—eggs over.

He got up, left a couple of silver dollars on the counter and stumbled out.

Soon he was back, poking his head in the door and yelling, "Anybody know where there's a good restaurant in this town?"

High Stakes Poker

This could have happened in any Montana town where it is rumored high stakes poker is played.

An inveterate poker player came into his ranch kitchen one morning to be confronted by an irate wife.

"Where in the hell is our pickup truck?"

"I lost it."

"You lost it playing poker?"

"Yep. I found out you don't bet on two pairs after the draw." Hardly able to contain herself, the wife asked, "How did you get home last night?"

"I rode Pete's horse home."

"How in the Sam Hill did Pete get to his ranch?"

"Oh, he didn't care. He was flying high, he won Luke's ranch. He probably stayed in town."

"He won Luke's ranch? My God, that ranch is worth a fortune. Where will his wife and kids live?"

"Aw, don't worry. When Pete sobers up, he won't remember what he won or lost."

Go with the Flow
Glimpses from the Golden Gulch

Dick Pace is the author of *Golden Gulch*, a fascinating historical account of discovery of gold in Alder Gulch and the birth of Virginia City and Nevada City. To make the present book more humorous, he has generously contributed several accounts of events and people in and around the Golden Gulch.

Tourists Loved Her

Zena Hoff came to the United States as a very young girl, probably in 1912 or so. After working as a maid for a while, she ended up on the stage, was with Pantages vaudeville on tour and then went to Hollywood and bit parts in Mack Sennett comedies.

From there she went to Catalina Island where she ran a gift shop and met a mining man. She toured the West with him, visiting almost every mining camp one can think of until they landed in Ramshorn Gulch here in Madison County. When he moved on, she stayed in Virginia City and eventually became a driving force in Charlie Bovey's restoration efforts. She found artifacts, designed the window displays and kept them clean.

There are dozens of stories about her, but one I treasure concerns a visit we made to the old Green Front, which Charlie was restoring as a railroad boarding house. This was after Zena was having trouble with her eyes so she asked me to take her down the boardwalk toward the depot where the Green Front is located.

My padlock key wouldn't work, so we had to peer in the windows. That done we started back up the boardwalk. Zena stopped after a few steps and said "Humph! Boarding house? Bed in every g.d. corner."

A few more steps, then "You know, kid, I wouldn't mind turning a trick or two. Hell, I'm too old. I'll be the madam and you can pimp for me."

By this time we had a sizeable crowd of tourists following us and listening in fascination to this little, old, gray-haired lady.

Between Raindrops

Lloyd W. Brook was Madison County's sheriff for almost 30 years. He looked as though he had come out of Central Casting: tall, with a prominent stomach and always dressed western style, but he never wore a badge that could be seen. Frequently he had it inside the flap on his western-style shirt.

Brook was a civic booster, especially with kids' projects. One day at the kids' annual fishing derby it was raining cats and dogs and I sat in the car with Brook between dashes into the rain to weigh a fish and take down the name of the kid.

After one such trip I said, "Won't this rain ever stop?"

Lloyd paused for a minute, then said, "That's the trouble with you kids, you don't remember when it rained 40 days and 40 nights, do you?"

A High-Powered Breath

Lawrence Grabinski has a cabin up Shafter Gulch at the head of Alder Gulch where he has a couple of mining claims. One year he asked Lloyd and Marvin Brook, sons of the aforementioned sheriff, to come up and help him with his assessment work.

During the first few days, the Brooks noticed Grabinski was a very methodical man, and noticed in particular how he laid his fire at night before going to bed. In the morning he would go outside, get some kindling, put it on top, then light a kitchen match and blow the flame through the side draft.

One night the three of them went into town and did a bit of imbibing, as a matter of fact quite a bit of imbibing.

The next morning Lawrence went through his normal routine, but while he was outside for his kindling, Marvin poured some coal oil on top of the laid fire.

Lawrence came back in, and put the kindling in and lit the match. Naturally when he blew the flame through the draft the coal oil took off. Stove lids flew up in the air and, as Lloyd Brook put it, Lawrence rattled around a bit.

But all the two of them did was sit at the table, shaking their heads and saying, "What were you drinking last night, Grabinski?"

Shaky Housekeeping

Sim Ferguson was probably one of the ugliest men one ever saw. A growth on his nose didn't add to his looks, and his arms, powerful ones, hung down below his knees. From all accounts he was tougher than nails.

He was married to an ex-madam called Bulldog Kate, and they moved into a cabin at the lower end of town. One day while Sim was sitting in the kitchen drinking his coffee, Kate took a pan of dishes to get some water to wash them. The pan slipped out of her hands and fell on the floor, breaking dishes like crazy.

Sim watched for a minute, then stepped outside, got an axe and started chopping up the furniture. Kate screamed and ran up the street yelling for help.

The undersheriff came down and told Sim he would have to go with him. On the way up town Undersheriff Pascoe said, "What in hell were you doing, Sim?"

"Well, if she wanted to bust up housekeeping, I was gonna help her."

A Paramount Mining Promoter

Andrew H. "Andy" Jones was a mining promoter to end all mining promoters. Among his many scams was this one.

He took a stoneboat and two oxen down to Sauerbier's Blacksmith Shop where he had Sauerbier start shoeing oxen.

This being a small town, people soon started drifting up to Andy to ask what he was planning to do. Andy told them he had made a deal with the monument works in Butte to gather up any grave markers that weren't paid for so the company could scrap them.

Soon people were coming in with $5, $10 or even $20 to pay on Uncle Harry's stone or Aunt Matilda's or somebody's. Andy stood there all day collecting money, then skipped town, leaving the stone boat and the oxen with Sauerbier.

Some Are Not So Blind

One of Virginia City's best known citizens was Bob Gohn. He was known all over the country as "the blind bartender." Bob, a third-generation resident, was blinded when he was 20. After a short despondent period, he started all over as a blind man, opening his own business in 1927 and remaining in business for the next 59 years until his death in 1986.

Everyone who knew Bob or had ever been in his place had a story to tell. I've got lots of them. One of my favorites is the night he got into an argument with Roy McClurg, Bovey's foreman at the time.

While they were arguing over the town's water system, Roy said, "I've got the plans at home. I can show them to you in black and white."

With a twinkle in his glass eye, Bob said, "No, you won't."

Roy kept insisting he could do it until he suddenly realized Bob would never see those plans in black and white or living color. When he got so mad he stomped out, forgetting the milk he had come to buy.

And, believe it or not, that glass eye could and often did twinkle.

1889
The Year That Wuz Montana's Birthdate
Century-Old Items from Montana Newspapers

A passenger from Great Falls to Fort Benton on a stage recently counted 25 wolves on the road over. No two-bit whiskey is sold in either of the places mentioned.

January 15, 1889
Butte Daily Intermountain

Who Won the Battle, Anyway?

The Custer National Monument has been so defaced that it will be necessary to recut the names on it. Indians riding by have made a practice of shooting at it, each ball doing its share toward marring it.

January 18, 1889
Butte Daily Intermountain

Author's note: Why is it called the Custer National Monument? Indians won the battle. There is a movement afoot to provide a fairer, more neutral name: The Battle of the Little Bighorn National Monument.

Is This a Shaggy Dog Joke?

PATIENT: "What is the best position in which to sleep?"
DOCTOR: "I usually lie down."

From the Fort Benton *River Press*

Pickup Rodeo Action

Roping and bronc riding was at Francis Bullshoe place and there were some good ropers and riders. One contestant came out riding his horse after a calf.

When he threw his rope, hit calf on the rump. The horse stopped quick. The rider fell forward and on down to the ground.

Guess he was too top heavy.

May 24, 1958
Glacier Reporter

Events of the Day

From the Great Falls *Tribune*—May 28, 1889:
"A balky horse delayed the Billings stage in starting today."

Ticket, Ticket, Who's Got the Ticket?

A swinging cowboy (if there were such characters 100 years ago) decided he needed some relaxation and caught the train to the nearest town noted for its night life.

According to the May 23, 1889 edition of the Great Falls *Tribune*, after he was seated, a conductor came along punching tickets. The cowboy paid no attention to him. Laying a hand on his shoulder, the conductor said, "Ticket, please."

The cowboy responded by pulling out a revolver, pointed it at the conductor and said, "Here's my ticket."

The conductor went on punching tickets and the cowboy dozed off.

Later the conductor returned and at a leisurely pace walked up the aisle to the cowboy. He placed a great big knife dangerously close to a vital part and said quietly, "Lemme see that ticket again."

The cowboy paid his fare.

Press Pot Shots Were Common

Editors and writers of Montana's Fourth Estate were wont to indulge in taking pot shots at politicians as well as contemporary newspapers and their editors.

Governors were not exempt either. The Butte *Intermountain* opined about Gov. Leslie's message to the opening session of the legislature that "The message is painfully long and might easily have been condensed into a single column without the omission of a single idea."

That was mild compared to the vitriolics bandied back and forth between newspapers of the day. How would you like to have your paper called a $2.00 harlot? The Butte paper stated: "The Anaconda *Standard* is a $2 harlot and itself is fond of calling other newspapers harlots. It ought to reform itself before it tries to reform its contemporaries."

The capital city issue was not settled until 1894, but on January 7, 1889, the *River Press* at Fort Benton reported that the head of Missouri river navigation might have a chance, stating, "Fort Benton will not proffer a claim for the capital, but with the complacency of a Christian behind four aces will sit back feeling fully assured that the prize will fall within our grasp."

The *Intermountain's* writers were not without a sense of humor. The paper observed that "the genial Tom Baker of the *Madisonian*, who was taken ill while in the act of making a pun and almost died trying to explain it to a friend, is convalescing and will hereafter hire a man to edit the humorous department of his excellent weekly and write the obituary notices."

Boodle, Booze & Silk Stockings _____

Elections to designate a state's capital city produce fireworks. At least Montana's did. The campaign was filled with bombastic oratory, charges and counter-charges, finger-pointing and exaggerations beyond belief.

In 1892, when Helena and Anaconda won the right to contest for selection as Montana's capital city, the stage was set for a bizarre campaign two years later.

Two copper magnates stage-managed the campaign. In one corner was Marcus Daly, who had built a smelter and the Montana Hotel in Anaconda. He was willing to put his money where his mouth was in promoting Anaconda as the site of the state capitol building.

In the other corner was William A. Clark, a long time mining adversary of Daly, who was determined that Helena, the territorial capital, should become the permanent seat of state government.

Boodle (money) and booze were alleged to be the "carrots" that were dangled to sway votes. As for the silk-stocking slur, this was pinned on Helena by the Anacondans, who contended that it was a campaign of the workingmen against the silk-stocking bunch.

To understand Montana's tumultuous 1894 campaign, one should be knowledgeable about what proceeded it.

After the gold strike at Bannack, it became the first territorial capital, to be succeeded by Virginia City following the Alder Gulch strike and the influx of a large population.

Helena made its first feint to move the capital out of Virginia City when boosters convinced the territorial legislature to submit the question of the capital city location to the voters. The election in September of 1867 gave Virginia City approval by a wide margin.

Helena's second try was made in 1869 when a bill was introduced in the legislature to move the capital to Deer Lodge. Somehow it was amended to read Helena. Again Helena went down for the count, but the record was besmirched by a series of odd events.

Ballots were accidentally burned before they reached Virginia City for an official tally.

Madison County, where Virginia City is located, apparently cast 1,800 votes for Virginia City, whereas the polling lists showed only 1,200 registered voters.

The Chouteau County vote was cast out entirely for reasons best known only to the election officials.

Such election jugglery produced signs in Helena reading:

"Lost, strayed or stolen—the seat of government. A liberal reward will be paid for its return to Helena. No questions asked."

Times were changing when Helena made a third bid in 1874. Placer mining was waning in Virginia City and Helena's State Street and Last Chance Gulch were crowded with miners, merchants, bankers and entrepreneurs, all part of a growing population.

The '74 campaign was bitterly fought with political fraudulence again showing its ugly face. The Gallatin County vote was thown out because of irregularity in making out the election reports.

More serious was the charge by Helena supporters that the Meagher County vote of 561 for Helena had been placed in the Virginia City column and only 29 votes credited to Helena. Not to be denied this time, the Helena adherents went to court.

The case was carried through the territorial courts to the United States Supreme Court, whence it was returned to the Territorial Supreme Court of Montana. Outcome was that a recount was ordered, to be supervised by a U.S. Marshal.

The revised tally showed Helena the winner by 561 votes, the exact opposite of that reported by the territorial canvassing board.

Despite burned ballot boxes, lost ballots, dead voters rising to pad registered voter lists, irregularities in election reports and switching of county totals, Helena's drive to become the territorial capital prevailed and the town remained so until 1889 when Congressional approval of a new constitution made Montana a state.

Eight contenders appeared in the 1892 race for the state's capital city: Anaconda, Bozeman, Boulder, Butte, Deer Lodge, Great Falls and Helena. With no clear victor after that balloting, the two highest vote getters were slated for a run-off election in 1894.

The cast of characters in the capital city embroilment was of a different lineup than those appearing in the Twentieth Century elections. Not so prominent were the political parties, chambers of commerce, and of course, PACS (political action committees).

Principal antagonists were newspapers, booster groups and prominent citizens with boodle.

Editors dusted off their finest prose, keened their phrases and honed flattering adjectives to an unprecedented degree.

Bozeman was described as the "Egypt of America" and a "dimple on the fair cheek of nature."

Its backers had their hackles raised when a communiqué from the Helena Boomers committee claimed Bozeman had withdrawn from the race and had hooked up with Butte.

Newspapers fired salvos daily. The *Montana Silverite,* a Populist paper in Missoula, wrote delicately of "The Hogocracy of Last Chance Gulch—the headquarters of Chinese laundries, gambling dens and opium joints."

On the drawing boards in the 1890s were all kinds of ghost railroads that never saw daylight. Railroads were a principal means of transportation and the major drawing card in the promotion of a city for the capital.

The Anaconda *Standard* stated, "Important fact is the Butte, Anaconda & Pacific railroad now under construction, which is to be extended to the Pacific coast, will be in operation to the west boundary of Montana within 14 months."

Fate, it seems, decided Anaconda to be the terminus and the BA&P never did reach the state's western boundary.

With voters in 16 counties casting 45,950 votes, the final 1892 results were as follows:

  Helena—14,010
  Anaconda—10,183
  Bozeman—7,685
  Butte—7,752

Great Falls, Deer Lodge and Boulder were "also rans" in the preliminary election to determine the finalists.

Next came a two-year circus. Montanans were treated to a spectacle—a vitriolic, gimcracky, sometimes blasphemous campaign.

Helena had a head start: It already was the territorial capital city. Transportation was in its favor—with two transcontinental rail lines, the Northern Pacific and the Great Northern, serving the city. And from a geographic standpoint, it was located closer to the center of the state's population.

Helenans proclaimed:

  Helena is a city—Anaconda is a village.

  Helena is everybody's town—Anaconda is one man's town.

  In Helena the people rule—in Anaconda the corporation rules.

Anaconda and the Dalyites had their comebacks, declaring "In the manufacture of lies she [Helena] stands alone and unrivaled...second to Helena's lying are her confessedly incomparable resources in gall, crude gall, assaying from 40 to 60%."

PACs were unheard of, but there were clubs. Women of Helena were organized as "Women's Helena for Capital Club." Miles City, in eastern Montana, got into the act with a "Custer County Helena for the Capital" club.

Gimmicks came into play on both sides. Baseball teams were

formed. Players sported either FOR ANACONDA or FOR HELENA on the backs of their uniforms.

The shadows of the two copper kings were everywhere. Daly had a specially twisted cigar rolled with a band reading "The Anaconda-for-the-Capital-Cigar."

There was a card handout (author unknown) reading, "I cannot Read or Write English, I Want to Vote for Helena."

Hat bands and ribbons lettered HELENA'S FRIENDS were prominent. Probably the most disparaging, lampooning piece of literature bore the title, *Helena's Social Supremacy.*

Its subtitle read: "Montana's Center of Fashion, Refinement, Gentility, Etiquette, Kettle Drums, High Fives [a card game], Progressive Euchre and Mixed Drinks."

The pamphlet stated:

The census of 1890 has been supplemented in some fields of inquiry by independent investigation on the part of the capital committee and the results are full of interest and edification.

Take for instance, the matter of silk stockings. In 1893 the consumption of silk stockings in Helena was 34,730 pairs, 3.387 pairs per capita, or 7.74 separate stockings per *legita*, a substantial increase over the consumption in 1892, despite the financial depression.

In Anaconda, the merchants do not even carry silk stockings in stock.

In Helena the percentage of claw-hammer coats to the total male population is 94.62; in Anaconda 13.83.

In Helena 87 persons out of every 100 say "trousers" and "waist-coats"; in Anaconda $98^1/_2$ out of every 100 say "pants" and "vests."

The following table taken from the *Helena's Social Supremacy* broadside was the real laugher. It stated, "it speaks for itself."

	Helena	Anaconda
Men who wear silk hats	2,625	3
Men who wear silk night shirts	2,910	4
Men who wear cotton night shirts	186	3,016
Men who wear overalls	0	3,220
Patches on seats of trousers	1	7
Patches on conscience	1,691	8
Dinner buckets in daily use	2	4,028

	Helena	Anaconda
Manhattan cocktails, daily consumption	17,699	127
Whiskey straights, daily consumption	13,303	1,977
Champagne (qts.)	1,245	2
Beers	4,088	8,854
Ladies who nurse their own babies	124	2,876
Ladies who do their own washing	8	980
Ladies who do the skirt dance	867	1
Ladies who can kick the chandelier	140	0
Ladies with poodle dogs	774	0
Ladies who give high fives	2,731	9
Ladies who rip other ladies up the back	1,296	147
Babies born with silver spoons in their mouth	435	0
Children who make mud pies	0	2,773
Horses with docked tails	1,182	0
Skeletons in closets	1,342	16
People who eat dinner at 6 o'clock	8,658	456
People who eat dinner at 12 o'clock	370	6,954

How is that for a poll before pollsters were discovered? Sarcasm was rampant throughout the campaign. Daly, the man, the Anaconda *Standard* stated, "walks the streets of Butte and Anaconda greeting friends in a $16 suit."

It contended that Daly was accused of controlling the Czar of Russia, was responsible for the Chinese-Japanese war and had caused the Johnstown flood and the Chicago fire.

The paper editorialized, "If Helena has not painted Marcus Daly's character as black as it deserves to be, let the fault be attributed to Helena's proverbial tenderness of heart and nobility of soul."

Boodle and booze were bandied about. A Hamilton paper raised the question, "Shall Boodle Win the War?"

The Anaconda Mining Co. and Marcus Daly were blasted for the corporation's expensive effort to win the capital city fight. It was alleged that Daly and the corporation spent about $2,500,000 or $50 per vote.

Apparently no estimate of Clark's expenditures was disseminated. Anaconda had an uphill fight and knew it. On November 6, 1894 the final election tally showed Helena the winner with 27,024 votes to Anaconda's 25,118.

The champ wasn't a winner by a knockout, that's for sure. But the campaign went down in Montana's history as a classic mud slinger.

To paraphrase an old axiom, "we shall not look upon its like again."

You'll Know You Are in Montana When...

...When a stranger greets you with a hearty "Howdy," or "Hi" or "How are you?"

...When you start up the Going-to-the-Sun highway in Glacier National Park, you are struck by the sparkling glaciers and massive mountains, and as you progress you become a believer that it is indeed God's cathedral.

...When you gaze upon Butte's cluttered, multi-colored landscape, you are not aware that you are looking at the "richest hill on earth" that produced more than a billion dollars in copper, silver, gold, lead, zinc and other minerals.

...When you stand astride the Continental Divide on Homestake Pass, you have one foot in the Pacific watershed and the other in the Gulf of Mexico watershed.

...When you wish to be more adventurous, climb Triple Divide peak in Glacier National Park, look around and you will see three watersheds—Pacific, Gulf of Mexico and Hudson Bay in Canada.

...When you see Square Butte and Crown Butte in central Montana, you will share vicariously in the thrill that Charlie Russell, Montana's premier western artist, experienced when he painted them.

...When you see the bison at the National Bison Range near Moiese, you can envision the vast herds of buffalo that roamed the plains and valleys of Montana.

...When you lie on your back and look up at Montana's sky, you will know why it is called the Big Sky Country.

...When you lightly flip a dry fly onto the surface of the Madison, Gallatin, Jefferson, Big Hole or Missouri river, you are fishing one of Montana's famous Blue Ribbon trout streams.

...When you are driving across the Fort Peck Dam in northeastern Montana, you are driving over one of the largest earth-filled dams in the world.

...When you visit the Headwaters State Park near Three Forks, you will stand in the footsteps of Lewis and Clark, the famous explorers, and view the three rivers—the Gallatin, Madison and Jefferson—as they form the mighty Missouri River.

...When you recall the year of 1889, it was not only Statehood year, but another Montana event that Montanans "busted their buttons over." They had a Kentucky Derby winner. A horse named Spokane, foaled at the now Bayers' cattle ranch near Twin Bridges, captured the Kentucky Derby.

*　　　*　　　*

Montana has a sense of serenity, a mosaic of color from its green burst of western mountain valleys to the Jacob's coat of browns, tans and reds found in its eastern badlands, coulees and gullies.

It is a state where you can hear a meadowlark (the state bird), enjoy wild flowers, rest your tired back against a sturdy tree and contemplate the benefits of solitude.

We have an unhurried life style, replete with breathing room, in our vast open spaces populated by friendly people.

All Sorts of Things and Weather

All sorts of things and weather
Must be taken together.

—Ralph Waldo Emerson

Without weather what would we talk about?

Without weather, unemployment would plague forecasters, television analysts, and rain and snow makers.

Without weather there would be a paucity of whopping weather tales.

Weather Forecasting by PS

There is a Montanan who relies on PS—Pig's Spleen—for his predictions. In case you are not knowledgeable about a spleen, it is a vascular, ductless organ near the stomach.

The spleen is often referred to as the seat of emotion. Pig spleens are as yet uncataloged.

"If the pigs' spleens are real thick and are out of proportion, it is a pretty good sign of a bad winter," says the forecaster.

In all probability the reader doesn't have a pig to split. Your next recourse is to look to Mother Nature.

There are those who watch antelope. If the antelope slip their horns early, it means an early winter.

Others gauge the length of hair on horses, or coyotes (if you can catch one). Long hair bodes a bad winter.

And don't forget the geese. Most of us learned in childhood that when geese start flying south, winter is on its way. "Not so," says an eastern Montana rancher. "If they are so danged high you can hardly see them, chances are that it isn't going to be a hard winter."

Confusion reigns when it comes to predictions of the other seasons. There is one sure sign of summer—sunburn.

Weather Whoppers

Montanans are not averse to discussing their anti-warm winters. They make jokes about it. The Helena *Independent Record* observed:

At Havre, it is said, fires were kept overnight by putting them outside every cold night, letting them freeze solid, and then thawing them out in the morning.

They say Miles City has mighty long winter nights because the dark gets froze so hard that daylight can't thaw its way through it in less than six months.

It is reported that when temperatures dip to 40 below zero recesses are not allowed at schools. Other frigid states might like to copy.

Recesses are not allowed because teachers are afraid the children would freeze stiff outside, that they would have to haul them in and lay them out in the hallways to thaw out.

Teachers are instructed to tell their children, when temperatures are so low, that when the sun is out to be sure your shadow falls behind you even if it means walking backwards.

That way you receive the benefit of the sun's warmth.

You better believe it's unbelievable!

Earthquakes Sire Mirthquakes

Humor in earthquakes? How gross! It is not the physical aspects of the quakes from which any semblance of humor springs. It is the human reactions to the earth-wrenching experiences that produce tragicomic incidents.

Eccentricities in time of stress are common. During the 1935 Helena earthquakes, I quaked through two major tremors and hundreds of shakes that started out the same way as the large ones. Mentally, these swarms of aftershocks were the incubation of trauma to many of the city's residents, myself included.

Reaction to the major October 18 quake, which measured 6.2 on the Richter scale, brought forth eccentricities galore.

The *Independent Record*, which reported a number of human oddities in the 50th anniversary edition on the earthquakes, cited "a dazed, naked man [who] stumbled down the street with an alarm clock in his hand."

An engineer inquiring of the desk clerk at the Placer Hotel for a room was told, "Take your pick, they are all empty."

Or the bartender in a South Main saloon, who was in the midst of drawing a draft beer when the building began to shake, made a rapid exit with the tap wide open, producing the only sudsy floor in Helena.

There was a stranger who ordered a cup of coffee in a cafe and had just finished putting in a spoonful of sugar when the shaking started.

He said to the other fellow at the counter, "This sure is an accommodating town. They even stir your coffee for you."

Then there was the government official who was working late at the office when the quake hit about 9:30 that evening. The lights went out, his desk did a jelly roll and his fountain pen slid to the floor.

He spent the next half hour crawling around the floor trying to find his errant pen. In the meantime, his wife, at home, was frantic. The house had developed an unexpected, and unordered, picture window when the front wall fell out.

Today there are matrons in the city who are superstitious of the sixth dance at a ball. When it comes up, they ask their partners, "Do you mind if we sit this one out?"

Their uneasiness is a remembrance of the sixth dance at the annual girls-ask-boys autumn ball at Intermountain College. It was about to begin when the building went into a rock and roll event that wasn't on the program. In total darkness they made their way outdoors through a rain of bricks and mortar. Luckily, no one was hurt, but the memory lingers on.

Big-game hunting season was on when the second major quake occurred at about 11:30 A.M., October 31. The *Independent Record* printed what happened to three hunters.

"They split up late in the morning. When they met again, one had been tossed down a hillside by the quake, the second had hugged a tree for dear life and the third, unaware of the shaking, had bagged an elk." How's that for concentration?

Schools closed, liquor stores closed and gas was rationed to five gallons per car because car owners sought mobility rather than sit in a house shimmying with aftershocks. The liquor store closing was a boon to bootleggers—they raised their prices.

One of the most interesting oddities printed by the paper concerned a tired miner who returned home after the October 18 quake oblivious to his house's damage:

Later concerned neighbors went in to wake him. They

shook him and told him he ought to get out where it was safe.

"To hell with the earthquakes," he said. "If the Republicans were in we wouldn't be having them."

And he rolled over and went back to sleep. It all goes to show—politics never takes a back seat to anything.

Index to Whimsical Map of Montana

1. **Peek-a-Boo Caribou.** They are supposedly found in Montana's northwestern corner. Take a lunch, a big lunch. You may have to travel into Idaho and British Columbia to get a peek. If you don't see them, you will have had a good outing through beautiful, forested country.

2. **Flathead Lake Monster.** Flathead Lake is a monster of a lake and supposedly is home to an underwater monster. The lake is 35 miles long and is one of the largest lakes west of the Mississippi. According to periodic reports, the lake monster is equal to the fabled Loch Ness monster of Scotland. Some say it is a huge fish, a mammoth sturgeon. One observer told me he had seen it and it was at least 15 feet long, but his friend said, "I put binoculars on it and discovered his monster was a grayish canoe floating upside down."

I'm skeptical. I won't believe it until I see a mermaid astride its long neck racing a speed boat.

3. **Mountain Campus.** Not many colleges or universities can lay claim to a full-grown mountain. The University of Montana, at Missoula, is butted up against Mount Sentinel. What an appropriate name. What the old mountain has seen of college life since the "U" opened in 1895 would fill a book, maybe a whole shelf of books.

4. **Fort Fizzle.** Back in the 1870s, the Nez Perce Indians went on the warpath in Idaho and headed Montana way. Army regulars from Fort Missoula hastily started to build a log fort in Lolo Canyon. The Indians arrived, parleys ensued, all to no avail. Whereupon the Indians by-passed the fort by riding and walking along an adjacent mountain ridge. No jogging was necessary.

5. **Virginia City Nude Art.** If you are a fancier of nude art—voluptuous, curvaceous female paintings that adorned early day saloon walls—drop in at the Bale of Hay saloon. The paintings will not only recharge your batteries but will spice up your drinks.

33

6. **Nevada City.** In nearby Nevada City, there is a structure that should have been in Ripley's "Believe it or Not." It is a two-story Chic Sales house (outhouse to the elite) at the back of the Nevada City hotel. It will accommodate four occupants at a time. It is undoubtedly the most photographed object in the restored town.

7. **Axolotl Safari.** If you are the adventurous kind, you might seek out the axolotl, an odd creature that resides in the Blue Lakes of the Gravelley Range south of Virginia City. They are salamanders and have both lungs and gills, are said to be at home on land or in water.

Not all Virginia City residents accept the axolotl story. Neighbors were heard arguing. Said one, "You can peddle that bull to the tourists, but not to me. There are no such creatures."

A few years ago, an axolotl named Oscar lived in a bucket near the front door of the Virginia City museum to prove that axolotls are for real.

One morning Oscar was missing—stolen. The custodian and feeder of the little creature, Mrs. Sadie Farrell, was distraught.

"You have to feed them in a certain way," she said. "You have to buy hamburger, wad it to about the size of your finger, pinch it onto a string and hang it in the bucket.

"The axolotl will eat the floating hamburger but not if it sinks to the bottom."

Picky fellow, isn't he?

8. **Devil's Slide.** Five miles north of Gardiner is a red slash on Cinnabar Mountain, called the Devil's Slide. In *Montana: A State Guide Book*, a jingle tells the legend of the slide:

> Ages ago, one can easily see,
> The mountains had risen, the valleys had sunk,
> And old Mother Nature got roaringly drunk.
> The Devil, as drunk as the Devil will be,
> Slid to the bottom of Cinnabaree.

9. **Grasshopper Glacier.** How about a refrigerator full of frozen grasshoppers? Okay to a fisherman, but nix to the housewife. Really, Montana has a grasshopper glacier, an 89-foot cliff of millions of hoppers embedded in ice and snow. Grasshoppers flying over the glacier were chilled, fell and were forever embalmed. It's a nine-mile hike up a mountain out of Cooke City to the hopper burial ground. During warm weather, bring perfume; thaws free great numbers of hoppers resulting in decomposition, resulting in hopper stench.

10. **Beartooth Highway.** This mountain highway from Red Lodge through Cooke City leads to the southeastern entrance to Yellowstone National Park. En route to Beartooth pass is a switchback aptly

named the Mae West Curve. She would like you to "Come up and see me sometime."

11. **Powder River, Let 'Er Buck** has been a Montana rallying cry for many years. The Powder River is known as "400 miles long, a mile wide, an inch deep and runs uphill." It also is known as too thick to drink and too thin to plow.

12. **Paddlefish.** No, you can't take an oar and paddle a fish, but you might catch one of the spatula-nosed monsters out of the Yellowstone river in the Sidney vicinity. They can weigh up to 100 pounds. "Catch" is not the right word; they are snagged. Sidney observes a Peter Paddlefish Day annually.

13. **Railroad–Auto Bridge.** A bit of historical trivia. The bridge was located east of Fairview. Auto travelers used to share a bridge crossing the Yellowstone river with train travelers. Imagine, you are halfway across the bridge in your Model T Ford and you meet a train. What was left became known as the "tin Lizzie."

14. Thirsty? You can visit **Giant Springs** at Great Falls where there is plenty of water. The springs produces 388,000,000 gallons daily, enough to provide three or four cups of water every day for each person in the world.

15. **Egg Mountain**. Only the name is whimsical. Located west of Choteau, it is a rare find and is the site of an 80-million-year-old dinosaur nesting ground. To spark your imagination, how would you like to have seen a herd of thousands of duck-billed dinosaurs? They appear to have been buried in a volcanic mudslide. The area is owned by The Nature Conservancy organization.

16. **Buffalo Butcher Shop**. Thousands of buffalo were slaughtered here, a prehistoric killing site. You can see where buffalo bones were left over a 1,400-year period. The National Register of Historic Places lists it by the oddball name of "Too Close for Comfort Site" because it is dangerously close to the Milk River. Wonder if they sell buffalo bones at the nearby Havre Village mall?

The Beforehands

Montana has not produced a humorist of the stature of Will Rogers. But his friend, Charlie Russell, Montana's premier western artist, was no slouch when it came to humor and story telling.

Whenever they met, I am sure Charlie had a stock of anecdotes to match Will's droll humor. Charlie's wit comes forth in his illustrated letters and cards contained in the book *Good Medicine,* published by Doubleday and Co., Inc.

Will Rogers writes in the Introduction, "If he had devoted the same time to writing that he had to his brush, he would have left a tremendous impression in that line...he was a great story teller. Bret Hart, Mark Twain or any of our old traditions couldn't paint a word picture with the originality that Charlie could. He could take a short little yarn and make a production out of it."

To illustrate Charlie's sense of humor, I would like to reprint letters, or parts of letters appearing in *Good Medicine.* The first is addressed to his old friend George Speck.

In order to better understand these letters, as the Publisher's Note explains: Mr. Russell's own spelling, punctuation and spacing have been followed in cases where the letters have been reproduced in type.

Friend George: This sketch will show Im still in Cal. I was at the beach the other day and if truth gose naked like they say it dos folks dont lye much at the sea shore. A man that tyes to a lady down hear after seeing her in bathing aint gambling much. Its a good place to pick em but its sometimes Hell to hold em.

I havent met maney of my friends down here this trip but I havent called on the Jails yet. Saw Sportecus, hes still packing a hide full. He shuck hands with about four of me and said he was glad to see me. I don't understand how he keeps away from the snakes maby they dont come with this new moon. aneybody else but Sportecus would of had crockdiles riding hyenas by this time.

Your friend

C. M. Russell

In the letters contained in *Good Medicine,* Charlie displays many opinions to his friends reflecting his love of the open range and his association with cowboys and Indians.

Of bronc riders, he wrote his friend Guy, "an Injun once told me that bravery came from the hart not the head. If my red brother is right, Bronk riders and bull dogers are all hart above the wast band but its a good bet theres nothing under there hat but hair."

To "friend Sweet," Charlie wrote: "The older I get the more I think of the old days an the times we had before the benchland granger grabed the grass. There was no law against smoking sigeretts then and no need of a whipping post for wife beeters. The fiew men that had wives were so scared of loosing them they generley handled them mighty tender. The scarcity of the females give them considerable edg these days."

As for medicine to ward off the flu, Russell cited Jonny Rich of Lewistown in a letter to friend Con. "He says, last winter when flew hit this town the Doctor advised him to take three mouths full of booze a day to head off the sickniss to make sure how much hes taking Jonny measures a mouth full which he says is an even pint. He follows the doctors orders to a hair and the Flew never touched him. said he felt fine all the time but after about a month of this treatment he got to seeing things that aint in the natural history. One day he saw a Poler Bear sitting on a hot stove waring a coonskin coat and felt boots eating hot tommales."

One of my Russell favorites, which appeared in the January, 1986 *National Geographic,* was written by Bart McDowell, assistant editor, and was titled, "C.M. Russell—Cowboy Artist."

McDowell wrote, " 'There's a difference in whiskey—some's worse than others,' Charley observed. He knew his 'brave maker' or 'trade whiskey,' as they called the terrible stuff. If a man had enough of this booze, you couldn't drown him. You could even shoot a man through the brain or heart, and he wouldn't die till he sobered up."

A.B. Guthrie, Jr., author of *The Big Sky, These Thousand Hills* and many other fine books, is prone to touches of humor in his writings. When asked if he would add a humorous story to the present work, he sent me the following which he called a one-liner:

My one-time father-in-law, a hearty drinker though not a drunk, took too much aboard one night. His wife, who occupied a separate bedroom, became aware during the night that he was having difficulties negotiating the stairs and getting into bed.

The next morning over breakfast, she said, "You had quite a load on last night, didn't you?"

Spearing another pancake, he answered, "Yep. Should have made two trips."

Also there was humorist John Tatsey, who was a policeman on the

Blackfeet Indian reservation. He was a correspondent for the *Glacier Reporter,* a weekly newspaper published at Browning.

Former United States Senator from Montana and ambassador to Japan Mike Mansfield is an admirer of Tatsey's writings. He labeled him "the modern day Mark Twain" and noted that Tatsey "could chuckle at life's absurdities. He had a wry humor. He poked fun at life in general and we are the better off for it."

The following appeared in a Tatsey column in the *Reporter* and was placed in the *Congressional Record* by Senator Mansfield.

There was a story told in Heart Butte. When a fellow went up north to Calgary years ago he camped in timber. From there he left by pack horse and hung up his harness in a tree. He came back 20 years and looked around. No wagon but horses still there. He looked up the trees and there was his wagon on the top of two pine trees 30 feet up.

To me, Tatsey's reporting was the essence of homespun humor. Montana also has had governors with a sense of humor. J. Hugo Aronson was one of them.

He was the governor who said, "Columbus discovered America, but I discovered Columbus, Montana. A railroad bull [policeman] kicked me off a freight train at Columbus."

Born in Sweden, Aronson came to this country as a young man. He recalled having trouble learning English. More than once, I heard him tell the story he recorded in his autobiography, *Galloping Swede.*

Everyone has to eat. I watched people order their food, but used sign language again and again, sometimes getting food that I did not like. Then one morning I was able to say "ham and eggs" in English and I felt good.

Then a new found friend taught me the American word for ground meat—hamburger. I stayed awake all night pronouncing the word hamburger, hamburger, hamburger.

Next morning I tried it on the waitress who asked "On white or dark?" I became so puzzled I responded, "Ham and eggs."

Even today if I am in doubt about the food or what I eat, I order ham and eggs.

Bob Fletcher was another Big Sky humorist. He put his wit to work on the state Highway Department's historical roadside markers.

Bob's wry humor is very evident on these signs. On the one describing the hanging of sheriff and road agent Henry Plummer, he noted, "It tamed him down considerably."

On a marker near Wagner, his colorful language is a joy to read:

Take it by and large, the Old West produced some tolerably

lurid gun toters. Their hole card was a single-action frontier model .45 Colt revolver and their long suit was fanning it a split second quicker than similarly inclined gents. This talent sometimes postponed their obsequies quite a while, providing they weren't pushed into taking up rope spinning from the loop end of a lariat by the wearied public.

Then there was the fella who had the nom de plume of Neckyoke Jones. His real name was E. Howard Sinclair and he found favor with the livestock people in his columns appearing in the *Montana Stockgrower*.

He covered a wide range of subjects, mostly dealing with the New Deal and the halcyon days of the Great Society.

In his first published letter, dated May 1943, Neckyoke raised this question of his companion or campmate, Greasewood:

"Well how does this rationin work?" I inquired to know.

"Now take beef fer instance," sez Greasewood. "They tell me there is more beef than the XIT, Con Kohrs an' ol John T. Murphy an' the rest of the boys ever heard of.

"But for some reason ruther they ain't enough T-bones to go around—so, accordin' to the papers, all a feller can have is about two pounds a week, an' they are goin' to eventually grind all the beef up, mix it with soy beans, saw dust and sweepin's from the mill and make hamburgers and baloney—just like stock cubes to feed the Americans."

And last, but certainly not least, is Col. Joe Montgomery. I can attest personally to his brand of western humor. He was a very colorful individual who "cashed in his chips" in Lewistown at the age of 107.

Governor Ted Schwinden sent a tribute to his funeral, stating "Colonel Joe was older than the State of Montana, and with his passing we have lost a part of our history. But we have retained the heritage of humor and humanity that he left as his legacy."

That pretty much sums up what Joe meant to Montana. He was really funny. He attributed his longevity to "good bourbon, never lying and leaving women alone."

Friends interpreted that statement to mean he never lied to women about leaving any bourbon.

He was quite a predictor of presidential races. He contended, "I don't think I ever picked a wrong one."

Joe was on safe ground; there wasn't anyone around that old to challenge him.

There were and are many others who fall into the category of humorists. I wish we could have included them all.

Once Over Easy

Montanans love good stories. They like jokes. It's a tonic that has served Montana well.

Texans Learn About Fur-bearing Fish

Most people have never heard about Montana's fur-bearing fish, especially Texans.

While representing the state of Montana at a Dallas Sports and Travel Show with Howard Sharp, Wyoming's Travel Director, it was my pleasure to edify Texans about Montana's prized fish.

The fish grow fur because they are found only in deep, ice-locked lakes, high in the mountains. Because the lakes do not thaw until mid-summer, these fish have voracious appetites once the lakes are clear of ice. But they are finicky eaters and hard to catch.

A proven method is to wait until the moon comes over the mountain. Spread a row of succulent peas along the shore, become proficient on a ukelele and strum a haunting melody like "Down by the Old Mill Stream" or "Cool, Cool Waters." And wait for results.

First the fish's snout will break water for a good look, followed by a flop onto shore to take a pea. Pounce on him immediately or hit him or her over the head with the uke, and sure enough you've got yourself a trophy—a genuine Montana fur-bearing fish.

While in Dallas, Howard and I were interviewed on a talk show. He told about Wyoming's jackalope and I described Montana's fur-bearing fish. We told viewers that they could be seen at the Montana and Wyoming booth at the Dallas Sports Show.

It proved to be a bigger draw than we had expected. Crowds thronged about our booth to look at the idiosyncrasies of the piscatorial and animal kingdoms.

In my explanation to the show goers, I would recount the above story of Montana's famous fur-bearing fish. Upon conclusion of my talk, I would raise my right hand and proclaim, "So help me, that's the Texas truth."

Silence enveloped the crowd for a bit after which came laughter. Then the Texans, known for their braggadocio, would sidle away knowing they had been had.

A Duo of Cowboy Dancers

This is a reasonably true story. I was involved helping Bill Browning of the Montana Chamber of Commerce host four metropolitan outdoor writers on a fishing trip, covering several of Montana's Blue Ribbon trout streams.

A different species, the high-finned Montana grayling located in the upper Big Hole river, intrigued the writers. Trout fishing was good, grayling only so-so.

After dinner at Jackson, one of the scribblers, named Andy, asked, "Al, isn't there any night life in Jackson?"

I assured him there was. The others wanted to finish their notes on the day's fishing, so Andy and I strolled across the street to the only other bar in town.

Inside the small, square saloon was a sight that surprised me. Sitting on the floor, propped against the short bar, was a guy playing a fiddle. In the middle of the barroom were two men dancing with each other. They were dressed in high heeled boots, jeans and western shirts, and they wore cowboy hats.

"Who are these guys?" asked Andy as we sipped our first drink.

"Beats me! I never saw them before," I replied.

Andy was fascinated by two men dancing together in a western bar. "Are you sure you didn't hire these guys and set this up for us?"

I said, "No way. They must be two cowboys, or hay diggers, from surrounding ranches." It was haying time.

As the evening wore on, the fiddler fiddled and the dancers danced, and the drinks kept coming.

Finally, Andy, who had been eyeing the dancers all evening, said "You know that taller fellow is a pretty good dancer. Guess I'll go over and ask him to dance."

I made for the men's room in a hurry where I had a good belly laugh. When I came out Andy was dipping and swaying to a waltz.

And so they danced until the other cowboy cut in. This cut-in, cut-out performance went on for some time.

I wasn't in the mood for dancing and was about to go back to the lodge when Andy quit dancing and announced, "Let's go to bed, I'm all waltzed out."

A Mule Is a Mule Is a Mule

Dick Wheeler, an author and faculty member at Eastern Montana College, told me about an early-day incident at Fort Benton.

It seems there were many Indians in the Fort Benton vicinity and their presence made many of the residents nervous.

The contingent of U.S. Army regulars decided to exhibit a show of force. The soldiers hauled out a mounted howitzer, a very miniature cannon. It was often fired from the back of a mule.

The mule chosen for the honor had never had the gun fired from its back. The howitzer was hoisted to the mule's back with the muzzle aimed over its rump.

A crowd had gathered to watch the exhibition and the people were warned to move back as the fuse was lit through the touch hole. Buzzing of the lighted fuse frightened the mule, which began whirling around. Soldiers, civilians and all dove for cover as the muzzle circled the crowd.

No casualties were reported. The nervous mule was returned to a more sedate pastime, grazing.

Instant Pioneers

From a letter by author Joseph Kinsey Howard (in his papers at Montana Historical Society) on the prospects for construction of Hungry Horse dam in northwestern Montana, dated January 22, 1947:

> ...the towns of Hungry Horse, Martin City, etc. are flourishing. Their people must have brought some money from war work because they haven't anything else to live on. These towns are the youngest and brashest boom towns I ever saw. Martin City, for instance, is busily planning a "Pioneer Days" fete in the spring to honor its old timers, the town will be a year old then.

Forty years later the scene has changed. Now they are communities serving local residents and tourists coming from and going to Glacier National National Park.

No songs will be sung, no statues built, but the Hungry Horse boom towns served a purpose in the construction of an important dam and recreation area.

Laughs Among the Lewis and Clark Expedition

In discussing the Louisiana Purchase, probably the biggest laugh was on France. Napoleon needed deep pockets if he were to continue his European wars. And so, France in 1803 sold millions of acres stretching from the mouth of the Mississippi River to the Continental Divide for the munificent sum of $15 million. Hardly enough to make a dent in Montana's present budget.

Another laugher occurred when Congress appropriated $2,500 to finance the Lewis and Clark expedition to explore the Louisiana Purchase. Apparently it was sufficient, unless money was forthcoming from other sources.

In their early explorations, Lewis and Clark used a keelboat to navigate upstream the Missouri River. As Robert Fletcher points out in his *American Adventure* book, "propelling a keelboat was no idle pastime." It was either pushed or pulled upstream. Occasionally, with a fair breeze, a sail was set.

As Fletcher notes:

> Each boatman was provided with a setting pole equipped with a knob at the upper end which fitted the hollow of his shoulder. The men would set their poles on the river bed slanting downstream and walk aft in single file on the narrow deck strip pushing as they went. When the first man reached the stern, he would retrieve his pole and return to the bow to start again.

> ...There is a technical question involved in such procedure. At the end of the day had these stalwart gentlemen been riding upstream or walking downstream and if they walked downstream as fast as they rode upstream how did they manage to get anywhere?

It was no hot rod party either while engaged in pulling the boat. How do you haul on a big rope while slapping at a horde of mosquitoes? Or perhaps you had to sidestep a rattlesnake or two. Nor were moccasins any great protection when stepping on a spiny prickly pear cactus, of which there were uncounted numbers.

But not all was torture for the Lewis and Clark men. They celebrated the Fourth of July while camped at White Bear Island close to the location of the present-day Great Falls.

Patrick Gass's journal noted: "Thursday 4th. A fine day. A part of the men were busily engaged at the boat and others in dressing skins until about 4 o'clock in the afternoon."

That was when the celebrating began. But two things dampened their festivities.

First they "drank the last of our spirits" which they had hoarded all the way from St. Louis.

Secondly, a rainstorm put and end to the dancing. The men danced with each other. But soaked moccasins in slippery mud were not conducive to good dancing.

Maria Wood might have lodged a complaint had she known the Indian name for the Marias River, which Capt. Lewis named for his cousin Maria. She might have objected had she known the Indian name for this stream was "the river-that-scolds-at-all-others."

But there were men who were subject to embarrassment also. Capt. Clark elected to return via the Yellowstone River to rendezvous with Capt. Lewis at the junction of the Yellowstone and Missouri rivers.

In his journey down the Yellowstone in canoes and buffalo boats, he entrusted the driving of their horses overland to Sgt. Pryor, Shannon and Windsor. They quickly discovered they had a difficult chore. Some of the horses had been used to hunt buffalo and whenever they saw a herd of bison they took off—rider or no rider.

An additional man was assigned to the horse herders, a man named Hall. Capt. Clark said of him, "as he was necked I gave him one of my two remaining shirts, a pr. of Leather Legins and 3 pr. of mockersons." Although he was not exactly a properly dressed cowboy, it was all for naught.

Pryor and his party overtook Capt. Clark after he and his men had reached the Missouri. But something was missing. They had no horses. Raiding Crows had captured the horses. At Pompey's Pillar, the horse tenders had constructed buffalo boats (buffalo hides stretched over willow frames). A much easier mode of transportation than "forking a jug-headed Indian pony intent on mingling with every itinerant buffalo herd that crossed the trail," Fletcher noted.

He also observed that Capt. Clark, upon reaching the Missouri River, "camped in the same spot as in April of the year before. The mosquitoes were too much for them so they left a note for Capt. Lewis and moved down stream. Clark went ashore to shoot a big horn or mountain sheep but the mosquitoes were so numerous that he couldn't keep them off his rifle barrel long enough to take aim."

The trials, tribulations and laughter of the expedition ceased upon return to St. Louis where in time they became national heroes to the American populace.

A Forest of Distinction

It is doubtful that many Montanans ever heard of the Rock Springs National Forest located in their state. It does not appear on any official maps.

And yet, residents of Miles City and Jordan can tell you where it is located. You will be directed to drive Montana Highway No. 22 that stretches between Miles City and Jordan.

As you approach the Garfield County line, look hard ahead and you will see the Rock Springs National Forest—a lone cottonwood tree that lives where no other trees flourish. Rock Springs is a one-tree designated national forest.

Oldtimers are not sure if the tree was planted or just sprang up alongside the road.

It is said, that in the early days, travelers in buggies and stage coaches used to stop and water the tree a little bit.

The Advent of Steel Hosses

Back in the early '20s there was an abundance of automobile manufacturers that produced Appersons to Wintons.

Cars were numerous, but they weren't accepted by the old-time cowboy, who preferred a good horse under him.

Up in the Grasshopper Valley, a rancher drove into his yard one day in a big, cream-colored Marmon. The cowboys were loathe to look at it. After a quick inspection one of the cowpokes volunteered, "I'll bet a month's wages that I can beat you to the main road riding my horse."

The young poke wasn't dumb. He was figuring the five gates between the home place and the main road would slow down any car driver having to get out, open the gate and then close it so the cattle couldn't scatter.

The bet was made. The poke saddled his best horse. The rancher started his Marmon. Someone fired a six-shooter and they were off, the Marmon leading the way.

At the first gate there was no hesitancy, the rancher gunned his motor and crashed through the gate, knocking down posts and all. The Marmon continued its rampage through all of the gates.

When the cowpoke rode up to his boss sitting complacently in the Marmon, he opined, "Guess I won't get paid next month."

"That's right. Time will pass quickly while you are fixing all the gates."

—contributed by Walter Brundage, Dillon

Moose Milk Libation

Lasso a nice fresh moose the night before and feed her well, so she'll be in a kindly mood next morning. Use gallon mayonnaise jars for shakers. To make one gallon, use six whole eggs well beaten, 6 tablespoons of sugar, 2 or 3 handfuls of ice cubes and a quart of good bourbon. Fill up the jar with whole moose milk. Shake well and serve and start over. For fancy tastes it is nice to have a shaker of corral dust to flavor the concoction after it is poured. If too far from a good dusty corral, use nutmeg.

Bare Facts About Bear Hunting

While working for the U.S. Forest Service one summer, I became acquainted with a packer who handled a string of mules bringing food and other necessities to our fire guard camp.

The packer was a native of Missouri, the Show-Me State, and he was a spinner of stretched-out yarns. This is not to say that all Missourians are perverters of truths and embroiderers of facts.

Naturally, while encamped in the forest, the conversations at eventide would tend toward hunting and fishing.

One of his stories was about a hunting trip into the Ozarks. He and his hunting companion were stalking a buck deer without much success. They were tracking him along a high ridge, walking separately on each side.

The packer said he was crossing a wide-open, grassy slope when he saw the horns of the buck standing just beyond the slope of the mountain. He felt that if he advanced the deer would see him and get away. "The wind was in my favor," he recalled, "and luckily I had my 'around-the-corner' rifle with me."

When asked what he meant by his "around-the-corner," he told us that he had bent the rifle barrel ever so slightly so that it would shoot in a left-hand angle around a corner.

We knew what was coming.

"I planted my feet firmly, sighted carefully down the barrel until I had the deer's rack centered in my cross-hair scope. Then I held my breath and fired. The rack disappeared and I ran forward to see what had happened.

"Sure enough my 'around-the-corner' rifle came through. The bullet had hit him behind the right ear.

"My hunting partner was amazed at the shot, but I knew old Betsy—that's what I called the rifle—could do it."

We were amused by his tall tale well told. During his weekly visits, the old packer repeatedly told us about his experiences with bears—grizzlies, black or brown bears, it didn't make any difference, he never had any real trouble with them.

It was not long after his last visit that startling news came over the telephone line that connected the ranger station with all the lookouts and fire stations. The packer was missing. He hadn't arrived at his scheduled overnight stop.

Everyone liked the old jawer, and we were all concerned about his absence. Daylight came and the telephone jangled. The ranger announced to all that the packer had made camp very late.

He was unharmed but chagrined. The reason he was so late, the ranger recounted, was that he had been treed by a bear. He had sat up in the tree most of the day while the bear waited at the foot of the tree for a Missouri morsel.

It wasn't until near dusk that the packer's bell mare came clanking along and scared the bear away.

Yes, the packer embellished the story too, how he had eaten pine resin and chewed on needles to keep from getting too hungry.

From then on, we noticed, he didn't elaborate on the tree escapade. As a matter of fact, we barely could get him to talk about it.

Country Correspondents

If there are preferred places in heaven, they should be assigned to country newspaper correspondents. They are the "great communicators" in their respective, rural communities.

Country correspondence columns, to an outsider, appear to be a hodgepodge of people's names, interspersed with local gossip. To the local reader, the country correspondence is the "who, what, when and where" of their friends and neighbors.

Correspondents' weekly reports arrive in various dress. Some are written in "along hand" as it goes along and along until at times it takes a committee to decipher it. Others may be typewritten by the "hunt and peck" method with the text going awry. A good compositor is quickly able to correct spelling, introduce punctuation and make the copy readable.

On the Dillon *Tribune,* we had a jewel of a correspondent, Mrs. Tony Schuetz, who reported from the small mining community of Argenta. As can be seen from the following gems, she was a humorist as well as a reporter.

Mr. and Mrs. Henry Shafer took their daughter Billie Mae to Dillon Wednesday to receive medical attention for a toe infection resulting from a cut she got in their petrified fence.

Mr. Nelson from the Dillon postoffice was in town Tuesday. I didn't see him but I recognized his dog riding in the back of his pickup truck.

The Schuetz, Ward and Berry families went camping over in the Big Hole last week. The scenery up there is really something. But the mosquitoes and flies were biting so much better than the fish that they were forced to leave after four days. It is tough to be so busy scratching with both hands that you are unable to slap at the biters who are busy making new scratching places.

The Ward family departed for Long Beach Wednesday claiming they had gained pounds and pounds during their visit to Argenta. More than likely it is lung expansion from breathing our pure mountain air.

Mrs. Lee James and the reporter shopped in Dillon Wednesday afternoon. At least at 11:30 a.m. they are still planning on it.

This news writing is, in the reporter's case, something like talking to yourself. The last couple of weeks she ain't had much time to talk to herself so not much news.

By next week she may be back in the groove. Maybe.

Bottom Fishing

The Fishing Caste

Montanans take their fishing seriously. You can honestly say there is a caste system. (No pun intended.) It ranges from the worm dunkers, or garden hacklers, along with the corn and marshmallow soakers, to the fly purists who squirm in horror at the thought of using grasshoppers.

Among the fly fishermen, there are two layers of the caste—the wet flyer and the pure purist, the dry fly angler.

I have a friend, Jack DeYoung of Helena, who remembers the days when you didn't need a fly box stuffed with a rainbow of colored flies. He swears by two wet flies—the Royal Coachman and the gray hackle.

None of the Fan Wings, Parachutes, Bi-visibles, Bitch Creeks (tsk, tsk), Zug Bugs, Fledermous (I thought that was an opera), Sofa Pillows and Cow Dung—not smelly, really—for him.

He recalled fishing a western Montana lake where he caught a six-and-a-half-pound rainbow trout on a Royal Coachman fly. He had a battle royal to land the whopper with a fly rod.

All fishermen and fisherwomen are proud of their catches. My friend showed his prize catch to the proprietor of the resort where he was staying and the Prop., who ran a sporting goods store on the premises, asked if he could exhibit it in an iced show case.

Many Montana fishing folk dabble in the art of fly tying. The Prop. fancied himself an A-1 fly tyer because he tied traditional flies and exotic creations of his own.

Next morning my friend came by to admire his big fish resting on a bed of ice. Hooked in its mouth was a fly—not a Royal Coachman—but one of the resort owner's wild creations.

Not one to raise a ruckus, my friend went on his way thinking, Oh, well, it just leaves that many more fish I can catch on a Royal Coachman.

A Big Fish Is Shot Down

I know an ardent fisherman who landed a nine-pound trout while fishing one of Montana's Blue Ribbon streams—the Madison.

He was really excited about the catch because he wanted to enter it in the local hardware store's Big Fish Contest. Being Sunday, he put it in his freezer to await entering it the following day.

His business partner agreed to go with him to the weigh-in. The fish tipped the scales over 10 pounds.

"I didn't think that fish would weigh that much," he said. Little did he know that his partner, the night before, had sneaked into his basement, lifted the fish out of the freezer and poured buckshot into the fish.

The hardware store owner assured the fisherman he was almost certain to win the Big Fish Contest. None of the other entries was even close.

But his partner stepped up and said, "Don't be too hasty with your predictions. There is something fishy about this fish."

Whereupon he whipped out a knife, sliced open the fish's belly and out poured a stream of buckshot.

The angler was stunned. His dream of winning the Big Fish Contest had been shot down.

Are Fishermen Habitual Liars?

Habitually fishermen are considered liars, but scientifically are they?

When is a fish the heaviest? At streamside, after it is gutted or, probably, when the catcher describes to a friend?

None of these, writes Bert Lindler, a staff member of the Great Falls *Tribune.*

"Fish grow big by eating other fish," he writes. "The reason fishermen can't remember catching any small fish is that the bigger fish have eaten all their memories."

Lindler attributes a mathematical equation, which he states was developed by Ray Quigley of Great Falls, to disprove the contention that all fishermen are liars.

Here is the scientific equation for fishermen:

$PW = (MW - Y) \div 2$.

PW stands for Physical Weight

MW equals mental weight

Y equals the time in years since the fish was caught

Mental weight of a fish is nebulous. Lindler writes that Quigley contends that as soon as a fish is lifted from the water, its mental weight doubles. Consequently he subtracts one pound of mental weight for every year that has elapsed since the catching.

And because of the doubling of weight by the fisherman or fisherwoman, he divides the mental weight by two to determine its physical weight.

It may take some mental gyrations to find out the real weight of the fish your friend claims he caught weighing eight pounds two years ago. Subtract the two years, which leaves the physical weight at six pounds. In order to compensate for the doubling of the mental weight, divide the physical weight by two, and your friend's fish is only a three-pounder.

Lindler states, "I hope this proof establishes once and for all that fishermen are not liars. They are simply helpless victims of natural laws that have never before been explained."

Now let's see. I caught a 16-pound whopper out of Flathead Lake 10 years ago. Sixteen minus 10 is six, divided by two is three. Oh, no! I've got to dig out that photo to prove to myself that the fish was bigger then three pounds.

Izaak Walton, roll over, progress has caught up to us.

Rugged Individuals, We Are Us

A few years back, a fellow who wanted to keep alive the spirit of the West robbed the East Helena bank while most of its residents were watching the annual Vigilante Parade in Helena.

He made his get-away in true western style, riding his horse out of town, the saddle bags stuffed with cash.

The aforementioned Col. Joe Montgomery summed up the early-day Montanan by stating:

Where would you find tougher men with the bark still on, prettier women and nicer kids?

There were lots of sweet talking hussies, rawhide cowboys, pretty squaws who dance all night, bartenders who listened to your troubles, "honest politicians", red-mouthed lawyers, honyocker homesteaders, remittance men, sky-pilot preachers, pill-pushing doctors, Florence Nightingale nurses, hard-rock miners, bullwhackers, stagecoach drivers and the best damn soldiers in the best damn town, best damn state and the best damn country in the world.

And you were right, Joe!

Gone are the honyocker homesteaders, the bullwhackers and stage coach drivers, but Montanans retain a fierce independence and resent the warped perception of our state and its people.

I was shocked one day while chatting with a tourist in a service station. He was most complimentary about the state's scenery, but his traveling companion chimed in, "Yeah, it's okay for people with low I.Q.'s."

To which I almost replied, "Why don't you stick around awhile, it might improve yours."

The media's perception of Montana can border on the ludicrous to the insipid. This was amply demonstrated by the horde of media reps who descended on Boulder after the shooting of Patrick Duffy's parents. Because Duffy was a well known "Dallas" TV personality, the newshawks scrounged every bit of publicity, true or otherwise, that they could uncover.

Laughable reporting was all over the place. The media reps noticed that many vehicles had plug-ins and drew the conclusion that there were many electric cars in Montana. That's factual journalism? Guess they thought we had 175-mile-long extension cords to run those cars.

While the horde of news people jammed the small town of Boulder, it was big-game hunting season in the state. Hundreds stalked deer and elk, wearing the required orange jackets and caps. (These colors are intended to prevent hair-triggered hunters from mistaking a human for a deer.)

An out-of-state newsman drew the conclusion they signified drunks and asked a Boulder resident, "Why do all the drunks wear orange?"

A resident tartly replied, "So we can see them coming."

Then there was the reporter who wrote about our three-inch snowfall about that time. He reported that truck drivers were having trouble with the storm on the Interstate highway. So much so that they were stranded on the highway. To keep warm they were burning spare tires, a standard practice in Montana, he contended.

Outright bull! The temperature never got close to zero in that autumn snowfall. Wish he would come back and show us how to light a rubber tire in a snowstorm.

It seems reporters don't bother to check facts anymore. We boondockers ain't that dumb! All of us know that the Brooklyn Bridge really isn't for sale.

Genes must have played a part in rugged individualism. Our forebears had the right stuff when it came to ruggedness.

One of the early stories about a traveling salesman recounts his stay in a small town hotel during a severe winter. '

The hotel was built before the advent of insulation. None of the sleeping rooms was heated.

The salesman endured what he believed was the coldest night ever. Next morning he came downstairs and broke ice on the water pail to wash.

About that time a fellow who had been out feeding and watering his team of horses came into the hotel. Frost covered his eyebrows and long beard, and icicles hung down from the beard.

The salesman was astounded and exclaimed "My God, man, what room did you have?"

We are rugged, yet friendly, like the sign in a cabin in the woods that proclaimed:

> If you are hungry, grab a plate
> You have my best of wishes
> But jes before you pull your freight
> Be shore to wash the dishes.

Montana has had and still has a host of individuals labeled "characters."

A Centenarian With a Flair

Certainly, Col. Joe Montgomery was one of the characters. After living more than a hundred years, Joe knew that the time was nigh when he would "cash in his chips" and he made his plans.

First, he asked a friend to take him out to the Lewistown cemetery so he could pick the place where he wanted to be "planted."

"And as ever, there was a flair for the unusual—he was planted in Lewistown on Leap Year day," reported Zeke Scher, a personal friend and staff writer on the Denver *Post*.

He reported, "When the casket was opened, there was Joe resplendent in his favorite outfit, bright red shirt with multicolored—black, white and red—tie, a red sweater and bright plaid jacket with matching Tam-o-shanter. Pinned to his tam was an Oklahoma Land Rush button and pinned to his shirt was a Spanish-American War badge."

Joe wrote his own epitaph. It reads: "Col. Joe Joseph Tildon Montgomery, Pvt. U. S. Army, 1876-1984." The other side of the tombstone bears the inscription: "Col. Joe, soldier, gambler, landman and weather predictor. I never voted wrong. Powder River let 'er buck."

According to Ken Byerly, publisher of the Lewistown *News-Argus* and a long-time friend of Joe's, one of his last requests was, "I want people to be happy at my funeral. So, after my graveside service is over, I hope everyone will gather at the Yogo Inn's Center Mark room for a last drink on me."

Joe meant it too. He had arranged for the party before his death.

Joe is gone but his humor is not forgotten.

When asked why he had never married, he replied, "It just wouldn't be fair—make one girl happy and disappoint all those others."

His summation of his life was, "I wouldn't change anything if I had to live it over again. I'd just double it. No, I guess there were a few poker hands I wouldn't have called."

A Not-So-Dumb Town Character

Nearly every small town has what might be called a town jester. He or she is a local institution. Maybe it is the little old lady with the cart who finds treasures in people's garbage. Or it could be the town drunk who doesn't get mad when you dismiss his panhandling.

We had a town character in my home town. You couldn't miss seeing him. He was seldom without an overcoat, come winter, summer, spring or fall.

When asked in midsummer, "Why are you wearing an overcoat in summer?" he would reply, "Why do you wear an overcoat in winter?"

To which you gave the proper reply, "To keep the cold out."

Grinning, he would say, "That's why I wear an overcoat in summer—to keep the heat out."

Sid (not his real name) wasn't anybody's fool. Once in the days when they used horses to haul lifts of building materials to upper stories, Sid was approached to drive the lift team. He dickered, "I'll do it for a dollar."

He was paid the dollar and went to work. He drove the horse forward lifting the material upward. When it came time to bring the lift down, Sid did nothing. The boss hollered, "Sid, back up the horse and let the lift down."

"Nope," Sid replied. "You paid me a dollar to drive it forward, it's another dollar to drive the horse backwards."

Another story relates he was hired to work pushing a wheelbarrow full of bricks. He reported for work, but he had lightened the load by pushing the wheelbarrow upside down.

Sid did odd jobs all over town. He worked for the city sweeping streets. One of the local jokers stopped and watched Sid sweeping up the horse manure that was common in those days.

"Hey, Sid," he hollered, "if you don't sweep faster, I am going to bite your head off."

Sid leaned on his broom and replied, "If you do, you will have more brains in your stomach than you have in your head."

Touché for Sid. He was a master of repartee with anyone.

A Bar's Major Domo

From the days when roistering cowboys rode into frontier towns "to shoot 'em up" to the plush watering holes of today, saloons, bars, taverns and lounges have been prominent establishments of Montana's communities.

Montana: A State Guide Book, describes the establishment of an early-day saloon thusly:

Claude Carter [founder of Ekalaka] a buffalo hunter and bartender, was on his way to another building site, when his broncos balked at pulling his load of logs through a mudhole at this spot. Carter stopped the plunging animals. "Hell," he said, "any place in Montana is a good place to build a saloon."

It was named the Old Stand and Carter went on to become known as a Montana character.

In Western Vernacular

Montana Glossary

It pays to understand western colloquialisms. They brighten your conversation and confuse the unwashed. The following, with embellishments, were inspired by *Montana: A State Guide.*

A *dogie* isn't a misspelled doggie, it's a calf looking for its mother.

Riding the *range* has nothing to do with a stove.

Don't try using a *broomtail* to sweep floors. He might kick you because he is a range horse of dubious value.

A *ditch* isn't always a ditch. It can be a drink—bourbon and water. Where the water is not so tasty, it may be called a slough water.

Bronco busting—riding by the seat of your pants on a sunfishing horse without grabbin' the saddle horn.

Chaps (pronounced "shaps") are not related to the fellas you hang around with. Cowboys wear chaps to protect their legs while chasing livestock through brushy areas.

Tin pants aren't worn by virgins. Woodsmen wear them because they are heavy, stiff and waterproof.

If you are a bird watcher, a *nester* may mean a bird sitting on a nest. But on the other hand, a "nester" is a homesteader and this state had a lot of them in the early days.

Buffalo *chips* are energy efficient, they can be burned.

To a rodeo (not ro*day*o) rider, *show daylight* doesn't mean that dawn has arrived. It's the daylight between the rider and the saddle. Too much daylight isn't going to help the rider in his bucking bronco performance.

Hog leg—no pork here. Nothing but a six shooter in a holster strapped to a leg may be called a hog leg due to its form.

You are in a heap of trouble if you shoot a *slow elk.* It means you shot a rancher's cow, steer or bull.

A *boilermaker* only tends to get a boiler maker boiled. A potent drink called a boilermaker is a shot of whiskey and beer on the side for a chaser.

Fishermen and fisherwomen love to catch chinook salmon. But a better catch is a *chinook*, the Indian name for a warm wind that melts the winter's snow.

When you *pull freight*, to go away, it is time to say "So long."

Do's and Don'ts in a Big City

This advice is not relegated to Montanans only. It is useful to all western kinfolk who go to big cities for a visit.

• Never smile at strangers.

If you smile at a stranger, he will probably stop and talk to you and ask you for your wallet.

• Don't propose necktie partics.

If your car gets stolen in the Big City and they catch the thief, don't insist on stringing him up. Necktie parties are out. Hire a lawyer, they need the work.

• Trade in your pick-up truck.

Big City dwellers have stopped making trips to garbage landfills.

• Drop western money talk.

Don't use money terms with city people such as two-bits (25¢), four bits (50¢), and six bits (75¢). If you say, "I gave the doorman a two-bit tip," Big City friends will wonder where you bit him in two places.

• "Spuds" is a no-no.

City folk refer to them as potatoes. In Texas, they might think you were talking about spudding in an oil well.

• Don't carry money in your back pocket.

Too many pocket pickers. Better to stuff the bills in your Long Johns, providing it is winter.

• Be polite in elevators.

Take off your ten-gallon hats while in an elevator. City folk are pale enough without all that shade in an elevator.

• Watch out for scalpers.

Big city sporting events have ticket scalpers on the prowl. Don't buy from the first guy who says, "Psst! Have I got a bargain ticket for ya, only fifty bucks." Tickets are hard to come by so you peel off a fifty. You're in like Flynn until the ticket taker says, "Hey, buddy, this ticket is for next week's game." Always read the fine print.

• Combine talk is loose talk.

Don't brag about your combine harvester or harvesters. City dwellers think a combine is when Phillip Morris merges with General Foods.

• Night clubbing can be dangerous.

Be careful while out night clubbing. Don't sit and drink six or seven exotic drinks like Sazeracs or French 75's, stand up and shout "Wahoo" or "Powder River, Let 'Er Buck." Big city night club patrons don't take kindly to such a ruckus. Chances are you might be escorted out forcibly by a hulk of a man, in a tuxedo, who looks like an NFL linebacker.

- Pay for a parking space.

You won't find a free parking space for your car in a Big City. You may wind up in a parking ramp garage where an attendant parks your car and brings it to you. When the feller zooms your car down the ramp with tires squealing and the car scraping the walls at every turn—remain controlled.

Don't holler, "You little twerp, you scratched the paint off the right side of my car," after which you belt him in the kisser.

This will bring out the gendarmes and the legal beagles. In court, they will prove that you disfigured him for life, his sacroiliac has gone south, and his sex life is non-existent. The beagles may try to get their hooks on your south forty. It is better, pardner, to grind your teeth, take a big chaw out of your plug of tobacco and spit on the floor, when they aren't looking.

- Be careful of parking lots.

If you don't like parking garages, try parking lots. But in a Big City give the parking attendant only the ignition key to your car. Don't give him the key to the car's trunk, especially if you have your wife's ranch mink coat stashed in there.

- Conversation about oysters.

When the conversation turns to oysters, don't mention how you love Rocky Mountain oysters. Most people don't know what a Rocky Mountain oyster is. It is a lamb or calf fry (nuts to you) and it is a delicate topic of conversation.

With Tongue in Cheek, or, How to Bruise Montana History ————

History makes one shudder and laugh by turns.
—Horace Walpole

In the book's beginning you were warned there would be fabrications.

Because history is serious business, historians frown upon playing fast and loose with historical facts and personages. And yet, don't you suppose there are historians who wonder how our early-day historical figures might have disported themselves under different circumstances and under modern conditions?

For instance, William A. Clark, one of Butte's copper kings, probably was caught in the wrong time frame of history. After Montana became a state, Clark announced that he wanted to be a U.S. Senator from this state.

Selection of U.S. Senators was different then. The electorate did not vote; selection was by the Montana legislature.

With power and money, Clark stood a chance. He was smarter than to use the U.S. mails in buying votes, rather he chose an airlift through the transoms of a hotel stocked with legislators.

Had William A. Clark been time-warped into the federal income tax era, he might have had a tidy deduction for "campaign expenses."

What about John Colter, discoverer of Yellowstone Park, and Jim Bridger, who earned the title of one of the greatest liars of all time? Imagine the hit team they would have made on the talk show circuit of television.

Plummer's Hanging

And then there was Henry Plummer, sheriff and chief road agent, embodied in one person. What if he had wangled a jury trial instead of being condemned to death in absentia by the Vigilance Committee in Virginia City and hanged by the Vigilance Committee of Stinking Water and Bannack?

The Vigilantes were men of action. They were really the first Neighborhood Watch or Crimestoppers bunch.

It is barely possible that Plummer might have been able to talk his way into having a hometown trial.

Dimsdale, in his book *Vigilantes of Montana*, states, "Plummer was a man of most insinuating address and gentlemanly manners under ordinary circumstances, and had the art of ingratiating himself with men and even with ladies and women of all conditions....It was only when excited by passion that his savage instincts got the better of him and that he appeared—in his true colors—a very demon."

In Bannack, Plummer undoubtedly would have found a legal eagle to defend him and the trial might have taken a few unusual twists.

A witness for the defense might have testified: "We must take into consideration the female population of our town. Sheriff Plummer is quite popular with the ladies. My wife tells me that he is the best dancer in Bannack.

"His death would be a distinct loss to the social activities of the community."

Again the defendant's counsel: "With your permission, your Honor, I would like to introduce, as Exhibit A, a letter from Mr. Horace Hangover."

Permission was granted and counsel read the following letter: "We should go slow in condemning Sheriff Plummer. After all, he is a duly elected sheriff, sworn to uphold the law. Should you resort to the irreversible act of hanging him, Bannack could become the laughing stock of the West—a town that has the audacity to hang its duly elected sheriff."

A character witness for the defense might have testified thusly: "Judge, I am a neighbor of Henry Plummer and I am here to vouch for his good character. I never have heard Henry curse in front of women; I never have seen him kick a dog or beat his horse over the head.

"They say he is a gambler but I play pitch with Henry now and then and find that he is not a very good pitch player. He owes me $10. I hope you don't hang him until I have had a chance to collect."

And so the trial might have gone on with the defense counsel refraining from pleading that Plummer was suffering "temporary insanity."

After summations, the Judge might have asked the opposing attorneys to approach the bench, table, or whatever it was.

In a hushed voice, he probably said, "Boys, we've got a problem. Let's go over to Sam's place and get a handle on this."

Following heated arguments by the attorneys, the judge might have agreed to the following plea bargain:

"Henry Plummer, you have committed some dastardly deeds in your time but to hang you now would indeed be cruel and inhuman punishment. I therefore banish you forever from the territory and should you return you will be shot on sight."

Actually, it could not have happened. The Vigilantes were determined to bring law and order to the territory and they swiftly did.

Ironically, Plummer swung from a scaffold that he had caused to be built for hanging a horse thief.

C & B—Talk Shows Hit

Imagine two famous mountain men on the talk show circuit, namely John Colter and Jim Bridger.

Colter is the reputed discoverer of what is now Yellowstone Park; Bridger was a trapper, scout and the acknowledged greatest liar in the Rocky Mountains. At another time, they might have emulated Will Rogers and starred in a Broadway revue or become headliners on the Pantages vaudeville circuit.

On television they most certainly would have starred. No store-bought clothing, just their everyday work clothes-fur cap—maybe adorned with a feather—deer skin jacket and pants sporting a bit of Indian bead work and a pair of thick moccasins. Along with long, long hair and thick, thick beards. They were the real McCoys.

Colter became a national celebrity when he appeared in the salons of St. Louis and described how he had found a thermal area on a high plateau in the Rocky Mountains that was alive with boiling mud pots, steaming pools and spouting springs.

No one had ever seen such a sight. Many believed it didn't exist. The disbelievers called it "Colter's Hell."

Yet this lurid tale was true. He was describing what was to become the country's first national park—Yellowstone National Park.

John Colter first appeared on the Montana scene as a member of the Lewis and Clark party. Apparently liking what he saw, Colter on the return journey eastward asked for release from the expedition in North Dakota and returned to Montana to become a trapper. In his explorations, he was the first white man to wander into the wonderland of the Yellowstone country.

It was Bridger who corroborated Colter's story of the Yellowstone. He declared he had seen a column of water spouting higher then the Virginia City flag pole, which was 60 feet high. Knowing Bridger's propensity for exaggeration, not many came to believe such a land existed.

Not until 1870, when the Washburn-Langford-Doane expedition toured the area, were the wonders of the Yellowstone verified by a reputable group of men.

Discovery of Old Faithful geyser proved a clincher. With the verification, Colter and Bridger had been deliared, temporarily.

Colter's second frontier notoriety occurred while he was trading with Indians in the Three Forks area.

During an encounter, a fight ensued. His partner, Potts, was killed. Colter was captured, stripped of his clothing and given a chance to run for his life if he could outrace the Blackfeet.

Stark naked he ran. He ran barefoot through prickly pear cactus and sagebrush. He raced five miles between the Jefferson and Madison rivers. He escaped by plunging into the Madison and reportedly hiding under driftwood.

He lived to continue his exploring, trapping and story telling. John Colter was one hell of a man—dressed or undressed.

Jim Bridger—Raconteur

A remarkable man. Known all over the West as an explorer and guide. He could draw you a map of the country you were going through on a deer skin or buffalo hide. He is the reputed discoverer of the Great Salt Lake; he was the first white man to explore extensively the Yellowstone Park country, and his stories about Yellowstone were termed "national legend."

He liked books, but was unable to read. Having heard about Shakespeare, according to a biographical description in the *Montana: A State Guide*, he sat for days by the Oregon Trail until he found an emigrant with a set of Shakespeare. He then hired a literate boy at $40 a month to read to him. He memorized many scenes that he later quoted.

But when the boy reached *Richard the Third*, Bridger threw the book in the fire. "No man," he shouted, "could ever be that mean."

Any interviewer or talk show host or hostess would have had fun with Jim Bridger.

INTERVIEWER: They say you are a romancer. Are you?

BRIDGER: Sure, I'm a real lady killer. They all fall for me.

INTERVIEWER: No, no, I mean you are given to telling falsehoods or exaggerating the stories that you tell.

BRIDGER: I'll be damned. Just because I fancy up a story a mite, I'm called a liar. I never lie. If I do, they love it.

INTERVIEWER: You have attended several mountain men rendezvous. Tell us about them.

BRIDGER: Not much to tell. After a long confining winter, the trappers, traders and others liked to get together for a party. There was a lot of drinking, fighting and story telling.

INTERVIEWER: Were there women and sex at these gatherings?

BRIDGER: Of course there was. It was whiskey, women and song. What did you think mountain men were—monks?

INTERVIEWER: Jim, it was rumored that you were a squaw man, that you lived with squaws. Is that so?

BRIDGER: Now that's none of your goddam business. If you don't quit asking personal questions, I'm of a mind to ask you outside for a butt kickin'.

INTERVIEWER: Mr. Bridger, may I call you Gabe?

BRIDGER: Sure, lots o' people call me Old Gabe and lots called me other things too.

INTERVIEWER: Gabe, you mountain men were given to exaggeration. Don't you think your story about a glass mountain was stretching the truth?

BRIDGER: Now wait a minute! I saw a glass mountain. It had great magnifying powers. You could see elk feeding 30 miles away, I swear. And I swear a lot.

INTERVIEWER: What about your story of seeing a petrified bird?

BRIDGER: You don't know how to say it. It was a peetrified bird, sitting on a peetrified tree singing a peetrified song. I know you're a doubter, but believe me, you gotta see these things to believe them.

INTERVIEWER: Before we go off the air, tell us about your most harrowing experience.

BRIDGER: Don't know what you mean by harrowing. If that means hair raising, I guess it would be the time I met a grizzly b'ar snout to nose.

I came up a hill on a trail and on the other side a grizzly was approaching. When he neared me, he stopped, stood up high on his hind legs. I thought he was as tall as a young sapling tree. Grizzlies don't see too good and he stood there until he caught my scent. I was afraid he might charge. Right away I whipped out my tin watch, hanging on a thong. I began swinging the watch back and forth. The sun glinted on it and before long I could tell the grizzly, while watching the swinging watch, had lost his belligerence.

Then I sang him a little ditty, "Oh doody day, oh doody day, oh doody, doody day." I kept repeating and my deep baritone voice had an effect on the b'ar.

Before long the grizzly dropped to the ground and sat there. I know it is hard to believe but I had hypnotized a grizzly b'ar. I went down, scratched his ear, nudged him and hollered "Git." He gitted and I chalked that one up to my fine voice and valuable tin watch.

Foofaraws, or Ornamented Stories

Boom Town Taxi Dancers

Taxi dancing is usually associated with big city ballrooms, such as Roseland in New York City, not a boom town in Montana.

Life magazine's initial issue, dated November 23, 1935, featured a picture of the Fort Peck Dam, taken by the famous photographer Margaret Bourke-White, on its front cover.

The issue carried a photo of a group of taxi dancers in a saloon at Wheeler, one of the boom towns created by the $100 million work relief project to build Fort Peck Dam across the Missouri River. It was Depression days and the project attracted 10,000 workers.

In addition to Wheeler, a camp named for Montana's Senator Burton K. Wheeler, there were New Deal, Square Deal, Delano Heights, Park Grove and Wilson. The red light suburb was tagged Happy Hollow.

Let us imagine the story of a North Dakota farm girl who became a a boom town taxi dancer through sheer desperation to get a job. Let us eavesdrop as she tells it.

I was home visiting my parents for a few days when my high school best friend dropped in for a gabfest.

"Tell me about Fort Peck," she said. "You were there back when they were building the dam, but you never talk about it."

I was reluctant to talk about those days which weren't the "good, old days." It was hard for me to believe that people would understand our life style in a raw boom town like Wheeler.

Today you can drive across the top of the dam and look at the vast storage reservoir behind it. Located 18 miles southeast of Glasgow, it is the world's largest earth-filled dam, and it is designed to store a million acre-feet of water and be a flood stopper for the lower Missouri river.

There are no vestiges of the boom towns remaining. But with the thousands of workers hired, they had to stay somewhere near the job. Boom towns of tar paper shacks, ramshackle buildings and tents sprang up over the windswept sand flats adjacent to the dam site.

I reminded my girl friend what our prospects were back in 1934. I was 18 years old and had just graduated from high school. A high school diploma didn't guarantee us a job.

And I was tired of doing farm chores and having Ma constantly nagging, "When are you going to get a job?"

Fat chance of getting a job in the nearest town, which was six miles down the road. Most of its residents didn't know where their next potato was coming from.

We lived about 100 miles from Glasgow, and our local rag—newspaper to you—began running stories about this big dam that was being built near Glasgow, at Fort Peck.

Any shot in the dark was worth taking. Why not go to Fort Peck and look for a job? I could be a cafe waitress or clerk in a store, anything to get away from the farm and Ma's harping.

I confronted Dad. "Can you give me enough money for rail fare to Glasgow?"

That prompted a family argument. Pa was hoarding what little cash he had; Ma was adamant, she was tired of a full-grown daughter lounging around the house.

Pa drove me to the railhead and put me on the Great Northern train headed west. The most exciting adventure of my life had begun.

When I got to Wheeler, I made the rounds. They wanted experienced hash slingers, not amateurs. Jobs were hard to come by for a girl.

Somebody told me that I might get a job as a taxi dancer in one of the saloons, of which there were many.

I asked, "What's a taxi dancer?"

He says, "You dance with guys and get paid for every dance. Go over to the Wild Swallow and ask for Charlie Doll. He owns the joint."

I found the Wild Swallow, walked in and found Charlie Doll. Doll was no doll. He had a two-day growth of beard, shaggy eyebrows, deep-set eyes and a belly that did a Jello-roll every time he laughed.

Later I found out that Charlie had a heart of gold, at least a heart of silver.

He looked me over and said, "What ya want?" I told him. "Are you a good dancer?" he asked.

"The boys at our high school dances and out at Mac's barn liked my dancing."

"Okay. I'll give you a chance. Here's the deal. You get paid five cents per dance."

Don't laugh. In the Depression days, a nickel was a hard nickel, worth a nickel. Inflation to me had to do with balloons, not money.

He went on, "If you get the guy to buy you a beer for ten cents, you get a rebate of five cents outa each beer. Chub, my bartender, will keep track and pay ya when we close."

I didn't hesitate. I needed a job.

"You better get some low shoes, clodhoppers they call 'em. No high heels."

As I left Charlie hollered, "Wear something light and sexy. It gets pretty hot in here and the hours are long."

That evening I approached the Wild Swallow with palpitations. Never, never had I dreamed of taking a job like this.

The other gals were already there. None of them was a Jean Harlow. A petite girl, named Julia, was friendly and we talked before the stomping began.

When the combo—a piano player, saxophonist and drummer—struck up the music, a rush for partners started.

They weren't mining coal at Fort Peck. They must have been mining dust. My first customer was dust from his curl-topped head to his No. 12 shoes. I kept looking down, fearful of those No. 12's stepping on my clodhoppers.

We got through the first dance all right. Then another guy grabbed me and whisked me away. Guess the custom was: Don't bother to ask.

And so it went. Some guys were thirsty and I encouraged them. That extra 5¢ helped while I rested my tired dogs.

After a flock of beers, my bladder was bustin'. I knew there was an outhouse in back, but didn't want to to out alone. I asked Julia to go with me. We found the crapper all right, but it was occupied. Julia said, "Come on, do it any place." So we squatted on the prairie.

It was a half-moon night and before we were finished, two guys came out. One relieved himself alongside an old car and the other up against the dance hall.

I had never seen a man urinating before, much less his equipment. Goes with the job, I guessed.

As the nights went by, I found out being a taxi dancer was plain, hard work—long hours on your feet, guzzling beer when you didn't really want it and learning how to handle odd-ball dance partners. They fell into several categories:

The Galloper—he would grab you and take off like his shirttail was on fire. Always on the outside of the dance floor he galloped, round and round, and when the music stopped, I was ready for a shower.

The Bumper—the tough guy who took delight in steering you into another couple. I was always the bumper. If the bumpeed took offense, my bruiser would say, "Why don't we step outside and talk it over."

The Dipsy-doodler—always center stage, middle of the floor, that is where he operated. His forte was dipping you nearly to the floor or twirling you around until you got dizzy.

The Conversationalist—he didn't know how to dance. All he wanted to do is walk you around the floor and talk. "Do you think FDR will get reelected, sure hope so." He walked and talked and got his 10¢ worth.

The Propositioner—you no more than started to dance when he offered, "Jeez, it's hot in here, let's go outside and cool off." That's not what he had in mind at all. My counter offer was, "We aren't allowed to leave until a break. Buy me a beer."

The only bright light in my life turned on when Danny Engleson showed up. He looked a lot like the Scandahoovians in North Dakota—blonde, muscular and smelled rural, if there is such a smell. I liked to dance with him. He was a gentleman, none of the get-a-leg-in-between dancing or patting my buttocks. Oh yes, there were any number of guys on the make with the taxi dancers.

After several months, I went home for a week's vacation. I wish I hadn't. Ma was a regular prosecuting attorney. She didn't dare come out and ask if I were still a virgin, but she sure wanted to.

Instead she went on and on about the stories she had heard about the prostitution, drunkenness and free love that went on in those boom towns. She kept after me to corroborate it all. I didn't tell her much.

Before I returned to Wheeler, I told her I had a steady boyfriend named Danny. That seemed to ease her conscience considerably.

In those days, living with a guy wasn't a common occurrence. Neither was acquiring "relationships." But I can verify there was premarital sex, an item I didn't let Ma or Pa know about.

As the months wore on, the taxi dancers became pretty good beer drinkers. After all, that was part of our income. There was one gal, Babs, who was really the champ at downing beers. She liked the stuff.

One night Babs decided to set a beer drinking record. After she had drunk about 50, word spread through the dance hall that she was trying to set a record. Every guy in the place was ready to spring for a beer.

Babs said, "If I can down 60, that's three bucks, I'll quit." It was near daybreak when she gulped down the 60th. The Wild Swallow went bonkers. Guys slapped each other on the back and kissed the gals. You would've thought it was New Year's Eve. They spilled out into the street, letting the town know that a world's record for women's beer drinking had been set.

"I'm bloated," Babs burped. To her husband, she pleaded, "Walk me, or carry me home."

Later he told me that she "sloshed all the way home and she spent most of the night making trips to the outhouse."

Her feat was the talk of the town. Guess the *Guinness Book of World Records* was published in those days, but nobody had ever heard of it.

Her only lasting claim to fame was that it was mentioned in the *Life* magazine article about Fort Peck.

One afternoon Danny showed up unexpectedly and says, "Why

don't you play hookey and we'll go to Glasgow and celebrate?"

I didn't know what there was to celebrate. Jobs were ending and Old Man Depression was still hanging around.

As soon as the water glasses arrived, he hauled out a pint of moonshine and announced, "Here's to us—let's get married!"

Then he produced a little, black case, out of which he extracted a diamond engagement ring. The diamond was miniature, but I didn't care.

"When?" I squealed.

"My job ends next week, so let's hit for the farm."

"What farm?"

The sly guy explained, "I've been putting my wages down on a farm in the Sidney area. There's a house on it, but it needs a lot of fixin' and we can do that gradually."

I kissed the guy muchly and said, "We'll have to have the wedding at home. If not, Ma will kill me."

And so it was, we were married in the Lutheran church in my North Dakota hometown. Ma and Pa conceded Danny would make a good husband.

That is my story about my Fort Peck days. But I haven't forgotten them.

Occasionally, I sit on our back stoop and look out over our farm and recall those hectic days of building the world's largest earth-filled dam at Fort Peck.

That's when I get nostalgic and I mentally drink a toast—beer, of course—to my friends, the taxi dance gals of Wheeler, Montana.

Saddle Sores and 10,000 Haystacks

There is a beautiful, high basin ringed with mountains in south-western Montana called the Big Hole. It is cattle country. It grows an abundance of wild hay. So much so that it is known as "The Land of 10,000 Stacks."

The Big Hole is the home of the beaverslide stacker. It takes a back seat to none of the modern-day round bale stackers or the mechanical loaf stacker.

In 1908 the beaverslide stacker was invented by two Big Hole ranchers, and it still serves the purpose of forming firm, symmetrical haystacks that are the trademark of this premier cattle country.

Some years back one of the ranchers disputed the haystack figure, asking, "How do we know there are 10,000 stacks in the basin?"

One Saturday night when Fetty's bar in Wisdom was crowded with ranchers, they had a gathering, sitting around drinking and arguing about how best to find out if there really were 10,000 stacks in the basin.

The problem was how to prove it.

One rancher suggested they phone each rancher and ask him how many stacks he had.

That was immediately shot down when somebody said, "That party line is so noisy you can hardly hear over it."

Another chimed in that "you can't get a word in edgewise." The telephone idea went down the drain when one of the oldtimers said, "Not all the ranchers have phones anyway."

A half-potted guy offered, "Why don't we use a helicopter? Bet the pilot could count 'em all in a day."

A rancher's wife spoke up and said emphatically, "Hell no! Those heliocopeters [she meant helicopters] make so much noise they'd scare the cattle and run 10 pounds off every steer in sight."

Finally, as the night wore on, it was decided to hire a cowboy to ride the length and breadth to count the stacks manually.

They hired Slats Magruder, whose butt had pounded a saddle for many a moon.

He had his own ideas as to how he would make the count. He would start at the north end of the basin and work south, crisscrossing so he wouldn't miss any ranches.

Slats said he would keep a tally sheet much like they used to do at elections. He would make four up and down marks and then a slash for the fifth stack with a final total on each sheet.

Slats didn't know that, before he finished, he would have four saddle bags full of tally sheets.

The rancher contended his information was provided by the State Extension Service. So heated became the argument that a fight ensued and Slats got a tooth knocked out.

Since there wasn't a dentist in the basin, he was taken to Butte where a dentist inserted a false peg. That incident cost him three days of counting.

Another whimsy that slowed Slats was his penchant for fishing. He liked to slip down to the Big Hole River, armed with a pint of whiskey and dry flies, to try to catch the high-finned grayling, a fish almost extinct in Montana.

Catching grayling wasn't easy, nipping on the pint was, and in the late afternoon it was easy to lie on a grassy bank and sleep it off. There went another day.

All these delays didn't go unnoticed by the ranchers. About midway in his count, a committee of his employers approached one day and laid down the law to Slats.

"There will be no more drinkin', fightin' or fishin', Slats," was the edict, "or you don't get paid."

Slats got the message. He rode hard and steady. The tally sheets in his saddle bags increased.

One fine Indian summer day in late September Slats rode into Jackson, lugged four bags full of tally sheets, threw them on a card table in the Jackson bar and announced, "There are 9,982 haystacks in the Big Hole. Let's round 'em off at 10,000 and call it 'The Valley of 10,000 Stacks'."

While the customers whooped and stomped, Slats pounded on the bar and hollered, "Set 'em up, Charlie. I'm buying."

The Outriders

Following the explorations of Lewis and Clark in 1804-1806, trapping and fur trading occupied the hardy mountain men who traversed the Montana area.

Not until 1856 did the country come alive with immigrants when gold was discovered by the quarter-breed Indian Benetsee on a creek in western Montana. Surprisingly certain, it was called Gold Creek.

Big gold strikes followed at Grasshopper Creek (Bannack), at Alder Gulch (Virginia City) and at Last Chance Gulch (Helena), along with minor discoveries.

The magic words "gold in Montana" spread throughout the country. Gold seekers came from all directions: from back East where people sought to escape a Civil War, and from gold camps of California, Colorado and Idaho they poured into the Montana mining camps.

Among them, let us imagine a young man, whom we shall call O'Toole. He was from Minnesota and he had a "get-rich-quick" gleam in his eye. We would find his correspondence with a boyhood friend most interesting.

Helena
Territory of Montana
April 5, 1865

Dear Kitt:

I know you are wondering what happened to me and where I am. I left Minnesota in a hurry but I had reason to.

I hit out fer the west and lit in the Territory of Montana. Helena is an exciting town. There are all kinds of people here—miners, merchants, bankers, saloon keepers, polyticians, card sharps and prostitutes.

At night you can hardly git into a saloon. They are all packed with perrsons spending gold panned out of Last Chance Gulch. Helena's Main st. is crooked, on purpus they say. When a card player is caught cheatin he can make a quick gitaway down Main st. and not git shot in the back.

You've probably heerd of streets paved with gold. Helena's could be. And everybody is still lookin for what they call the mother lode. So am me.

When I first got here, I swamped out a saloon until I got a grubstake. Now I'm trampin the hills searchin for gold. I have a shovel and a pickaxe and go where where I think I might find a pocket of gold.

There is 2 kinds of minin here. Placer minin is where you take a pan and fill it with gravel or dirt alonside a stream. Then you fill the pan with water and slosh it aroun. Gold is heavy and stays on the bottom of the pan. The gold is in dust, flakes or nuggets.

The other kind of minin is called hard rock. You find a rock ledge or dig a hole and come up with rocks that contain flakes or streaks of gold. Now and then the rock will break off into nuggets. The rock is shipped to Wales, where they have crusher machinery to smash it. From the crushed ore they git the gold. How I don't know.

You won't believe it, but when it rains heavy and the water washes down thru the gullies and streets of this town people go out lookin for gold nuggets. And find 'em.

I'm tired of writin. Kitt, leave the farm and come west. The two of us can make a fortune here.

As ever your friend
Jamie O'Toole

Farbough, Minnesota
July 11, 1865

Dear Jamie:

Why in hell did you leave town in such a hurry? You must have had good reason but I'd like to know why.

I'd like to go west to. But I can't leave now. Pa has bought four more milk cows and I'm the chief tit puller. He's tryin to get a milk contract with a big creamery. If he does mebbe he will hire some help and I kin get away.

Write again. Or better yet, send me a nugget.

Your old buddy
Kitt

Helena
Territory of Montana
August 15, 1865

Guess your titled to know why I left. You remember I was goin around with Kathy Maguire? One night I got brave and asked her to marry me. Told her that I would be a wealthy man in a short time.

Remember her father owned the Luck of the Irish Brewery and probably still does. I figgered he would give me a good job or set me up in business.

When Kathy told her mither about me asking her to marry, the old gal blew her cork.

The next time I came callin she cornered me and shouted, "You rat go back to your hole or wherever you been livin.

"You are a miserable figure of an Irishman. You don't even wear green on St. Paddy's day."

I din't dare tell her that my family were Orangemen. That's why I hi tailed it out a town.

Time's awastin, Kitt. You can't imagine how rich some of the gold strikes are around here. A fella told me that about 20 miles from here up Confederate Gulch a newcomer struck one of the richest finds ever made in these parts. His claim, called Montana Bar, was less than 2 acres and it yielded about $1,000 a pan when washed. Altogether 2 million dollars in gold was takin from the claim. Sure wished I could find somethin like that myself.

Buy yourself a ticket on the steamboat to Fort Benton. Quit pullin those cows tits, there's plenty of others out here.

No nuggets until you get here.

Jamie

Farbough, Minnesota
Sept. 10, 1865

You sure were out of your class tryin to marry Kathy. She's engaged to a sport from Minneapolis.

I'm still sittin on eggs. Pa can't make a deal with the creamery. He's payn me wages now and I'll hav the money to head for Montana when I kin get away. I wish our cows would get constipated. I'm tired haulin out their crap.

Not much to report around here. Your letters are most interesting, especially the part about findin all that gold nearby.

Keep writin—it gives me hope.

Kitt

Helena
Territory of Montana
Sept. 30, 1865

Dear Kitt:

You gotta git out here soon. I'm crackin up. I did the dumbest thing the other day.

I was wandering over the hills up behind Helena near a town called Unionville. I was follerin a crick down hopin to see some color and Lordy there it was. Beavers had dammed the crick and formed a small pond. All around the pond was a sort of black sand and in the sand were flecks of gold. There were millions of them!

I pan washed quite a bit of the sand and took it to the assay office where they test for gold. I couldve died when the guy looked at the flakes and said, "That's not real gold, that's fool's gold. They are mica flakes."

That's me, a fool. I'd never heered of fool's gold. I was so shook up I went to me room and just sat there for the rest of the day. What a stupid mistake.

But I'm not going to quit prospecting for gold, real gold. It's all around here. Wish you would hurry up and git here. The two of us can cover more ground and double our chances of strikin gold.

Yours for real gold
Jamie

Farbough, Minnesota
Oct. 18, 1865

Dear Jamie:

Halleluiah. You're goin to see me afor long. Pa's deal is goin through. Gonna take about a month then I will head west. I'm acomin!

Your Partner—Kitt

Helena
Territory of Montana
Nov. 2, 1865

Dear Kitt:

Sure glad to hear your headin Helena way. I need help. Right now I'm in jail. It's all a big mistake.

I was out prospectin yestiday when I came across a horse out in the wilds. He din't run away, let me pet him and put a rope around his neck. I sure can use a horse to carry my equipment and grub.

I led the hoss home and put him in a stable. Today a big slob fella and a man with a tin badge came lookin for me. The guy with the badge said he was the sheriff and the big fella claimed I stole his horse. Steelin horses in this country is a serious crime. They used to hang horse thieves. I'm hopin they aren't planning a necktie party for me.

I told the big fella it was a mistake. I din't intend to steel his horse. I told him where his hoss was and he could have him back. He let out a string of cuss words and said he'd like to beat my brains in.

I'm hopin my landlady will see the light and bail me out or pay my fine. As for horses, I'm goin to leave them alone until we strike it rich. Then we'll buy a pair of blacks and a good lookin buggy and ride down Main st. Bet we can pick up gals with a rig like that.

Hurry up, I'm waitin.

Your pal—Jamie

Loot of the Innocents

I am one of the Shades, a disembodied spirit who inhabits Hades. I also am one of the Innocents.

The Innocents were a loose organization of evil men who robbed and murdered miners and citizens during the gold rush days of the early 1860s in southwestern Montana.

Rich gold strikes on Grasshopper Creek brought about a miner's camp at Bannack. Another rich strike in Alder Gulch produced Virginia City. They were about 90 miles apart—slow, tiresome miles on horseback or in a jolting stagecoach.

There were plenty of places for the Innocents to hide and wait for the lonesome rider or the stagecoach with its load of well-heeled passengers.

We knew what we were doing. We had a good spy system. All kinds of people—express employees, clerks, stable hands, bartenders, gamblers and prostitutes reported to headman Sheriff Henry Plummer the goings and comings of people with pokes of gold dust or strong boxes filled with gold and money.

There were plenty of mysterious disappearances because our people knew where to look for them. We had a code that really worked. It was marked on men, horses, wagons and coaches, a telegraph system to the watchers.

We were known as road agents and highwaymen.

We worked well together. Our rendezvous places were several. One was at Rattlesnake Ranch. The best known was Robber's Roost, six miles down the road from Virginia City. Actually it was a stage station known as Pete Daly's place.

With a barroom, where you could get "Tangle-leg" and "Lightning"—throat-searing whiskey—and a dance hall, it was a great place for connivin' and celebratin'.

During our reign of terror, when apprehended, we always stated

"I am Innocent." This slogan was swept to the winds when 24 of the Innocents, myself included, were hanged by the Vigilantes.

Besides our cipher system, there were other ways we fingered those who had struck it rich.

Card games went on night and day in Virginia City and Bannack. Kibitzers usually stood around the tables. A tipster might have said, "Too bad, Ray, losing on a pair of aces." Pair was the key word, meaning two, which meant the victim was about to leave via route two.

Or one of the Innocent card players might accidentally, or on purpose, drop a card from his hand on the floor, whereupon a tipster would hurriedly stoop to pick it up. As the Innocent bent low to retrieve the card, the tipster might whisper, "So-and-so is leaving tomorrow for Virginia City."

Even in barrooms messages were relayed.

At Robber's Roost, an Innocent might come in, spot another Innocent and invite him over to the bar for a drink. He might order a two-finger, three-finger or a "filler up" drink.

Two fingers meant their intended victim would be heading south to Bannack.

Three fingers meant he was going to Hellgate (Missoula) via Deer Lodge.

And a "filler up" order signalled he would be on a coach destined for Helena. In a quiet corner, the Innocent would be told their pigeon had made his fortune and wanted to get out of the territory and return to his eastern home.

There was no shortage of tipsters, take it from one who listened to many of them. Some were paid money. Others were told "Keep your eyes and ears open and your mouth shut or else you may witness a murder—of yourself."

Now and then a loner would hold up a rider on the trail and keep the money for himself.

I recall a lone, masked road agent who lifted a sizeable poke from a miner riding between Bannack and Virginia City. After he had sent the miner packing down the trail with the admonition "Don't try to figure out who did this or you might get a bullet in your back," he began looking for a place to hide his loot.

He spotted a clump of cottonwood trees at a distance from the trail and he made for it. Under a big cottonwood, he dug a deep hole between the roots and buried the poke. He carefully replaced the dirt, then scattered leaves, grass and twigs over the dirt. To be certain he would recognize the tree, he cut a big slash in the bark.

When he returned to collect his loot, about six months later, he started cussing violently. During the summer lightning had struck the tree, or an adjoining one, and the entire grove of trees had burned. Only blackened scarecrows remained standing. The poke is there, if you can find it.

Innocents didn't lack ingenuity when it came to hiding places. There was a member whose horse stepped in a hole, broke his leg and the Innocent had to shoot him. That left him with a hike over the Ruby Range to reach Virginia City. Three bags of dust and nuggets strapped around his waist, he found, were cumbersome in his mountain walking.

He looked for a hiding place and found it. He came across a spring hidden in heavy brush. Divesting himself of the bags, he let them drop to the bottom of the spring. For recognition, he made a small circle of rocks nearby.

After spending a few days with a friend of his, drinking heavily each day, he got into an argument over the favors of a dance hall girl. A shootout occurred and he came out the loser, never to return to his secret spring.

Maybe, some day, someone will come across a golden spring, for surely by now the bags have rotted away and the bottom of the spring is paved with gold. Verily, it may be the pot of gold at the end of the rainbow.

I am not a stool pigeon for the Innocents. There were rumors that several of my co-conspirators had buried their loot at the Point of Rocks, a prominent landmark between Twin Bridges and Dillon. There are some who call the promontory Beaverhead Rock.

Whatever its historical name is, it has not yielded the golden treasures of the Innocents. Recently rocks and gravel were being hauled from its base for road building. With that much activity, the hidden gold should have come to light.

I don't want to start a snake stampede, but there are numerous rattlesnake dens in southwestern Montana.

They would be perfect hiding places for bags of gold and strong boxes filled with coins, bills and dust. I am not saying the Innocents hid their loot in rattlesnake dens, and I'm not saying they didn't.

While on vacation from my place of torment, Shade-like I wandered among the scenes of my downfall, and I did spot a gold-colored rattlesnake glittering in the setting sun. Could be that a bag or box broke open, after all these years, and the snake had slithered through the dust.

I have heard that rattlesnakes like to snack on gold as an aid to their digestive systems.

Should you come across a big, gold rattlesnake think twice before you kill it and have it mounted as a trophy in your den. On second thought, just think how much a solid gold rattlesnake would be worth at today's gold prices.

Or you might choose to have the dead rattler cut up into snake meat steaks for the reptile gourmets. Don't sell too cheaply. A three-ounce rattlesnake steak, marbled with gold, should be worth around $1,200 with gold selling in the neighborhood of $400 an ounce.

If you go snake den hunting, be careful, take others with you. I know about a snake hunting posse in the Dillon area. It had a great chain of command, from the leader down to the "pickup man."

The leader selected the den. Then the snake snatchers went to work with their long poles and nooses. When a snake was snared, it was dropped in a containment arena. There the "pickup man" patrolled the area and herded any strays back into the holding place to await their demise by a well directed bullet.

The question still remains: "Where did the road agents hide their stolen gold?"

We can sit in our hell-hole and smirk. Much of the gold was squandered on booze and women. But goodly amounts were hidden, and they may never be found. Like the Lost Dutchman mine of the Superstition Mountains in Arizona, which has never been found, neither have any great amounts of the Innocents' gold.

In retrospect, I guess we Innocents got our comeuppance. In our Hades homeland, we are shunned as thieves, desperadoes and murderers. Our crimes are far more serious than those of many of our neighbors.

Even the Devil hasn't forgiven us. He has relegated us to the outer circle, which is away from the fires of hell. We are allowed to cook on one side and freeze on the other. He teases us with his taunts, "Where is the gold?"

We know, but we are not about to squeal to the Devil. We say, "To Hell with him!"

At Trail's End

The Fun Bunch

Life has its vagaries. One day you are up, the next day maybe down. But among Montanans there runs a strain of friendliness which, like an injection of adrenalin, gives you a pleasant "attitude adjustment."

Your day becomes brighter because of the warmth and candor of your fellow citizens.

There are exceptions, but Montanans are a fun bunch, even when the going gets tough.

At times they do crazy things.

NBC got a charge out of coming to the state to film a TGIF (Thank God It's Friday) segment for the *Today* show a few years back.

It was mid-winter. NBC producers discovered that Martin City residents sponsored a bar stool race. A bar stool race on skis. You strap a bar stool onto a pair of skis and race down hill. Most contestants wound up as rumper-bumpers. Their claim to fame was they appeared in a bar stool race on NBC.

NBC also filmed a fellow water skiing on Flathead Lake with the temperature near zero degrees.

When asked why he did such a goofy stunt, he was serious when he said, "I got a new boat for Christmas and I was just trying it out."

Montanans' humor has been with us since the first mountain man short-sheeted his partner's bear skin sleeping bag.

"Yup," as Gary Cooper was wont to say. Montanans like to leave you laughing.

Albert Erickson was born in Hamilton, Montana. He has a journalism degree from the University of Montana and is a graduate of a U.S. Army public relations school at Washington and Lee University, Lexington, Virginia.

He was a Montana Tourism Director in the administrations of Gov. John Bonner and Gov. J. Hugo Aronson.

He and his wife, Dorothy, were owners and publishers of the Dillon, Montana *Daily Tribune.*